Real Food
from just
One Pan

Carol Palmer

foulsham
LONDON • NEW YORK • TORONTO • SYDNEY

foulsham

The Publishing House, Bennetts Close,
Cippenham, Berks, SL1 5AP

ISBN 0-572-02500-9

Printed in Great Britain by Cox & Wyman Ltd, Reading

CONTENTS

INTRODUCTION

One-pan cookery still seems to remind us of 'one-pot' cookery and with it the image of bubbling stew pots suspended over open fires attended by either ancient dames or enthusiastic Girl Guides! This book will banish that picture forever and give a whole new meaning to the concept of cooking in one pan. The recipes illustrate that the pan may be anything from a grill (broiler) or frying pan (skillet) to a steamer or casserole (Dutch oven). The important common factor is that the whole dish is cooked within that one vessel. Add a simple accompaniment and you are ready to serve.

Cooking in one pan does not just mean casseroles and stews, but a vast range of dishes cooked by a whole host of cooking methods. There are guaranteed to be recipes here to suit all tastes, and dishes range from the exotic to 'good home cooking'. Some recipes are quick to cook – such as some of the stir-fries and rapid desserts – and others may take a little longer but allow the cook to be getting on with something else while a roast or casserole is doing its own thing.

The essence of these one-pan recipes is that you can produce delicious, modern and stylish meals quickly and easily. With only one pan to cook in, the dishes are economical on time, equipment, labour and effort! That makes them ideal for the cook who likes to eat well and experiment with new recipe ideas while expending as little time and energy in the kitchen as possible. The same qualities also make them perfect for those new to cooking (they are straightforward but give encouragingly great results), those with limited facilities and equipment (because you don't need a fancy kitchen), and those who simply love food (because the finished results taste great!).

Real Food from Just One Pan adopts a realistic approach to cookery, respecting the fact that most of us do not have the time or money to cook dishes that require us to shop for hard-to-find or expensive ingredients. However, it also takes into account that today's cook is in constant search of new flavours and ideas while having a good understanding of the importance of nutrition and diet. This is why the recipes rely heavily on a sensible combination of storecupboard ingredients and fresh foods. There is no sin in using cans and packets as long as they are balanced with fresh ingredients and the nutrients, colour, texture and specific flavours they provide. The recipes call for a range of ingredients to create a wealth of flavours – savoury and sweet – with a worldwide feel, but you should find that all are readily available from a well-stocked supermarket. Many of the dishes are very adaptable and allow adventurous cooks to substitute ingredients that may be more suited to their own personal tastes.

Real Food from Just One Pan is the cookery book everybody should have, not just to use on the days when you are feeling lazy and don't want to get all the pots and pans out of the cupboard, but for every day. Whether you're preparing a family meal, a dinner party or an evening snack, you'll find a wide range of great eating for everyone.

YOUR ONE-PAN STORECUPBOARD

If you want to create dishes quickly and easily with the minimum of effort, you must have the right ingredients to hand, and the best way to ensure this is to have a well-organised and well-stocked storecupboard. Not so long ago, a storecupboard contained little more than packets of dry goods, such as flour, sugar and rice, but nowadays, with the benefit of home freezers and modern packaging methods, we can keep many canned, dried, chilled and frozen items in our kitchens, ready for use.

On the following pages you will find a comprehensive list of those ingredients I consider to be most useful, plus a few that apply specially to recipes in this book. You may wish to add your personal favourite items, and don't forget to replace things as you use them.

DRIED/PACKETS

◇ Flour: self-raising (self-rising) and plain (all-purpose)
◇ Cornflour (cornstarch)
◇ Bulgar (cracked) wheat
◇ Couscous
◇ Egg noodles
◇ Baking powder
◇ Sugar: caster (superfine), demerara and soft brown
◇ Rice: long-grain and arborio
◇ Pasta, any shape
◇ Suet, shredded (chopped)
◇ Polenta (cornmeal), instant
◇ Cocoa (unsweetened chocolate) powder
◇ Dried milk (non-fat dry milk) powder
◇ Dried pulses, including lentils
◇ Sultanas (golden raisins)
◇ No-soak prunes
◇ Chopped nuts
◇ Ground and flaked (slivered) almonds

CANS AND BOTTLES

◇ Canned tomatoes
◇ Sun-dried tomatoes
◇ Passata (sieved tomatoes)
◇ Canned pulses
◇ Stoned (pitted) olives: black and green
◇ Canned fruit, particularly peaches and pineapple
◇ Canned tuna
◇ Bottled lemon and lime juices
◇ Cartons of orange and apple juice
◇ Canned evaporated milk

HERBS, FLAVOURINGS AND CONDIMENTS

◇ Peppercorns: black and green
◇ Salt
◇ Mustard powder
◇ Wholegrain mustard
◇ Stock (bouillon) cubes: vegetable, chicken, fish and beef
◇ Tomato purée (paste)
◇ Garlic purée
◇ Soy sauce
◇ Worcestershire sauce
◇ Vinegar, including balsamic
◇ Cooking oil, including extra virgin olive oil
◇ Dried herbs, including thyme, oregano, rosemary, marjoram and tarragon
◇ Spices, including ground cinnamon, turmeric, garam masala and paprika, cinnamon sticks, whole nutmeg, bay leaves
◇ Curry paste
◇ Pickles and chutneys, including mango
◇ Plain (semi-sweet) chocolate
◇ Honey, clear
◇ Golden (light corn) syrup
◇ Jam (conserve) or jelly (clear conserve), particularly redcurrant

REFRIGERATOR AND FREEZER

◇ Eggs
◇ Milk
◇ Butter
◇ Margarine
◇ Cheddar cheese
◇ Cream cheese
◇ Grated Parmesan cheese
◇ Mayonnaise
◇ Cream: double (heavy) or whipping, single and soured (dairy sour)
◇ Plain yoghurt
◇ Frozen puff pastry (paste)
◇ Frozen filo pastry
◇ Frozen sweetcorn (corn)
◇ Frozen peas
◇ Frozen chopped herbs, including parsley, mint and coriander (cilantro)

◇ Do not mix metric, imperial and American measures.

◇ All spoon measurements are level: 1 tsp = 15 ml;
1 tbsp = 15 ml.

◇ Eggs are medium unless otherwise stated. If you use a different size, adjust the amount of liquid added.

◇ Always wash, peel, core and seed, if necessary, fresh fruit and vegetables before use. Ensure that all food is as fresh as possible and in good condition. Clean all meat and fish appropriately before cooking.

◇ Always use fresh herbs where possible, but if it is necessary to use dried use half the amount stated. Chopped frozen varieties are better than dried. There is no substitute for fresh parsley and coriander (cilantro).

◇ Can and packet sizes are approximate.

◇ Use any good-quality oil, like sunflower, corn or groundnut (peanut), unless olive oil is specifically called for.

◇ Use appropriate butter or margarine of your choice in the recipes.

◇ Use your own discretion in substituting ingredients and personalising the recipes.

◇ Use whichever kitchen gadgets you like to speed up preparation and cooking times: mixers for whisking; food processors for grating, slicing, mixing or kneading; blenders for liquidising.

◇ Always preheat the oven and cook on the centre shelf unless otherwise specified or using a fan-assisted oven.

◇ All ovens vary, so cooking times have to be approximate. Adjust cooking times and temperatures to suit your own appliance, especially if you have a fan-assisted oven.

◇ Cream or yoghurt, or a mixture of the two, may be substituted for crème fraîche. Do not allow crème fraîche to boil.

SOUPS AND STARTERS

Soups are the ultimate in one-pan cookery – they're simple and quick to prepare and need little or no attention once the ingredients are in the pot. The selection I've given here includes Minted Tomato Soup (see page 12), a light and subtle variation on a familiar theme, and Libyan Lamb Soup (see page 15), which is hearty enough to be a meal in itself. The other starters are just as varied, with suggestions to suit every occasion, from a quick lunch to an elegant supper party for friends.

MINTED TOMATO SOUP

—— SERVES 4 ——

	METRIC	IMPERIAL	AMERICAN
Butter or margarine	30 ml	2 tbsp	2 tbsp
Large onion, finely chopped	I	I	I
Large carrot, grated	I	I	I
Celery sticks, finely chopped	2	2	2
Ripe tomatoes, skinned and chopped	I kg	2¼ lb	2¼ lb
Chopped fresh mint	60 ml	4 tbsp	4 tbsp
Vegetable stock	600 ml	I pt	2½ cups
Milk	600 ml	I pt	2½ cups
Tomato purée (paste)	15 ml	I tbsp	I tbsp
Brown sugar	15 ml	I tbsp	I tbsp
Freshly ground black pepper			
Salt	7.5 ml	I½ tsp	I½ tsp
Greek yoghurt, sprigs of fresh mint and crusty bread, to serve			

① Melt the butter or margarine in a large saucepan, add the onion, carrot and celery and fry (sauté) gently until transparent.

② Add the tomatoes and 30 ml/2 tbsp of the chopped mint and simmer for about 15 minutes until soft.

③ Add the stock and milk and cook for a further 10 minutes.

④ Add the tomato purée, sugar, black pepper to taste and salt.

⑤ Allow to cool slightly, then liquidise or purée to make a smooth soup.

⑥ Return to the pan, stir in the remaining chopped mint and reheat gently.

⑦ Pour into warm soup bowls, add a swirl of Greek yoghurt and a sprig of mint to each and serve with fresh crusty bread.

PREPARATION TIME: 20 MINUTES
COOKING TIME: 35 MINUTES

QUICK LEEK SOUP WITH GARLIC AND HERB CHEESE

—— SERVES 4 ——

	METRIC	IMPERIAL	AMERICAN
Butter or margarine	15 ml	1 tbsp	1 tbsp
Oil	15 ml	1 tbsp	1 tbsp
Large leek, very thinly sliced	1	1	1
Large onion, very finely chopped	1	1	1
Tub of garlic and herb soft cheese	125 g	4½ oz	1 small
Water	600 ml	1 pt	2½ cups
Vegetable stock (bouillon) cube	1	1	1
Cornflour (cornstarch)	15 ml	1 tbsp	1 tbsp
Milk	300 ml	½ pt	1¼ cups
Salt and freshly ground black pepper			
Garlic croûtons, to serve			

① Heat the butter or margarine and oil in a large saucepan, then add the leek and onion. Cook gently for about 10 minutes or until very soft.

② Stir in the cheese, then gradually blend in the water. Crumble in the stock cube and bring the mixture to a steady simmer.

③ Blend the cornflour with a little of the milk, then stir the paste into the remaining milk and add this to the saucepan. Stir well and cook until slightly thickened.

④ Season generously with salt and pepper.

⑤ Pour into warm soup bowls and serve with garlic croûtons.

PREPARATION TIME: 10 MINUTES
COOKING TIME: 25 MINUTES

APPLE, CHEESE AND WALNUT SOUP
—— SERVES 4 ——

	METRIC	IMPERIAL	AMERICAN
Cooking (tart) apples, peeled, cored and roughly chopped	450 g	I lb	I lb
Water	600 ml	I pt	2½ cups
Sweet white wine	300 ml	½ pt	1¼ cups
Strong Cheddar cheese, grated	225 g	8 oz	2 cups
Walnuts, finely chopped	75 g	3 oz	¾ cup
Salt and freshly ground black pepper			
Crusty bread, to serve			

① Place the apples and water in a saucepan and bring to the boil. Reduce the heat, cover and simmer for about 15 minutes until the apples are very soft.

② Use a hand blender or potato masher to crush the apples to a smooth purée.

③ Add the wine and return to the heat to heat through.

④ Stir in the remaining ingredients.

⑤ Pour into warm soup bowls and serve hot with fresh crusty bread.

PREPARATION TIME: 10 MINUTES
COOKING TIME: 15 MINUTES

LIBYAN LAMB SOUP
—— SERVES 4 ——

	METRIC	IMPERIAL	AMERICAN
Extra virgin olive oil	15 ml	1 tbsp	1 tbsp
Garlic cloves, crushed	4	4	4
Large onion, finely chopped	1	1	1
Lean boneless lamb, very finely chopped	225 g	8 oz	8 oz
Passata (sieved tomatoes)	150 ml	¼ pt	⅔ cup
Can of lentils, drained	400 g	14 oz	1 large
Ground cinnamon	2.5 ml	½ tsp	½ tsp
Ground cardamom	2.5 ml	½ tsp	½ tsp
Vegetable stock (bouillon) cube	1	1	1
Boiling water	600 ml	1 pt	2½ cups
Salt and freshly ground black pepper			
Plain yoghurt	90 ml	6 tbsp	6 tbsp
Chopped fresh mint	30 ml	2 tbsp	2 tbsp

1. Heat the oil in a large saucepan, add the garlic and onion and fry (sauté) gently until very soft.

2. Stir in the lamb and cook until well browned.

3. Add the passata, lentils and spices and stir well.

4. Dissolve the stock cube in the water and add to the saucepan. Season to taste with salt and pepper and heat through.

5. Combine the yoghurt with the mint.

6. Pour the soup into individual bowls, swirl in the yoghurt mixture and serve.

PREPARATION TIME: 10 MINUTES
COOKING TIME: 20 MINUTES

MEXICAN SOUP
—— SERVES 4 ——

	METRIC	IMPERIAL	AMERICAN
Olive oil	15 ml	1 tbsp	1 tbsp
Medium onion, chopped	1	1	1
Garlic clove, crushed	1	1	1
Can of Mexican refried beans	450 g	1 lb	1 large
Vegetable stock (bouillon) cube	1	1	1
Boiling water	600 ml	1 pt	2½ cups
Passata (sieved tomatoes)	60 ml	4 tbsp	4 tbsp
Tomato purée (paste)	15 ml	1 tbsp	1 tbsp
Sugar	5 ml	1 tsp	1 tsp
Salt			
Finely chopped bottled jalapeño chilli peppers	30 ml	2 tbsp	2 tbsp
Strong Cheddar cheese, grated	60 ml	4 tbsp	4 tbsp
Tortilla chips, to serve			

① Heat the oil in a large frying pan (skillet), add the onion and garlic and fry (sauté) over a low heat until lightly browned.

② Reduce the heat and stir in the refried beans. Dissolve the stock cube in the water and gradually stir into the bean mixture.

③ Add the passata, tomato purée, sugar and salt to taste. Stir well and bring up to simmering point.

④ Stir in the chillies and simmer for a further 5 minutes.

⑤ Pour into individual bowls, sprinkle with grated cheese and serve with tortilla chips on the side.

PREPARATION TIME: 5 MINUTES
COOKING TIME: 15 MINUTES

LUXURY PORT AND STILTON PÂTÉ

—— SERVES 4 ——

	METRIC	IMPERIAL	AMERICAN
Ripe Stilton cheese	225 g	8 oz	8 oz
Port	30 ml	2 tbsp	2 tbsp
Cranberry sauce	30 ml	2 tbsp	2 tbsp
Crackers and French bread, to serve			

①   Mash the Stilton well.

②   Beat in the port.

③   Stir in the cranberry sauce and mix until well combined.

④   Pack into a pâté bowl and chill.

⑤   Serve with a selection of crackers and French bread.

PREPARATION TIME: 5 MINUTES

COOKING TIME: NONE

GRILLED VEGETABLES WITH CHEESE SALSA DIP

—— SERVES 4 ——

	METRIC	IMPERIAL	AMERICAN
Red (bell) pepper, seeded and cut into long thick slices	1	1	1
Yellow pepper, seeded and cut into long thick slices	1	1	1
Courgettes (zucchini), cut into long thick fingers	2	2	2
Medium aubergine (eggplant), cut into long thick fingers	1	1	1
Canned baby sweetcorn (corn) cobs, drained, or thawed frozen	12	12	12
Chilli-flavoured oil	30 ml	2 tbsp	2 tbsp
Garlic cloves, crushed	2	2	2
Jar of cheese salsa	290 g	10½ oz	1 medium

1. Preheat the grill (broiler) to medium and line the grill pan with kitchen foil.

2. Arrange the vegetables over the foil.

3. Combine the oil with the garlic and brush all over the surface of the vegetables.

4. Place the vegetables under the grill and cook until they are tinged brown and slightly softened.

5. Turn the vegetables over and brush with the remaining oil, then return to the grill and cook until tinged brown and just tender.

6. Serve the salsa in a dish placed in the centre of a large platter, surround with the vegetables, and dip away!

PREPARATION TIME: 15 MINUTES
COOKING TIME: 10 MINUTES

BULGHAR WHEAT WITH PRAWNS AND MANGO

—— SERVES 4 ——

	METRIC	IMPERIAL	AMERICAN
Bulghar (cracked) wheat	225 g	8 oz	2 cups
Boiling water	300 ml	½ pt	1¼ cups
Grated lime zest	10 ml	2 tsp	2 tsp
Lime juice	15 ml	1 tbsp	1 tbsp
Spring onions (scallions), thinly sliced	4	4	4
Can of mangoes, drained and diced	400 g	14 oz	1 large
Cooked peeled prawns (shrimp), fresh or thawed frozen	225 g	8 oz	8 oz
Chopped fresh parsley	15 ml	1 tbsp	1 tbsp
Balsamic vinegar	30 ml	2 tbsp	2 tbsp
Extra virgin olive oil	30 ml	2 tbsp	2 tbsp
Salt and freshly ground black pepper			
Lime wedges, to garnish	4	4	4

① Place the bulghar wheat in a large bowl and pour the boiling water over. Leave to soak for 30 minutes until the wheat is soft, then pour off any excess liquid.

② Combine the wheat with all the other ingredients, seasoning to taste with salt and pepper.

③ Serve in individual bowls, garnished with lime wedges.

PREPARATION TIME: 15 MINUTES PLUS 30 MINUTES STANDING TIME
COOKING TIME: NONE

SWEETCORN AND MUSHROOM DELUXE

—— SERVES 4 ——

	METRIC	IMPERIAL	AMERICAN
Butter	25 g	I oz	2 tbsp
Olive oil	15 ml	I tbsp	I tbsp
Garlic clove, crushed	I	I	I
Shallots, thinly sliced	50 g	2 oz	2 oz
Button mushrooms, sliced	225 g	8 oz	8 oz
Can of creamed sweetcorn	250 g	9 oz	I medium
Cayenne	2.5 ml	½ tsp	½ tsp
Salt and freshly ground black pepper			
Bread and butter, to serve			

① Heat the butter and oil in a medium frying pan (skillet) and add the garlic and shallots. Cook gently until they are transparent.

② Add the mushrooms and continue to cook until they are soft.

③ Stir in the creamed sweetcorn, season with the cayenne and add salt and pepper to taste.

④ Heat through gently, stirring occasionally.

⑤ Serve hot with slices of fresh bread and butter.

PREPARATION TIME: 5 MINUTES
COOKING TIME: 5 MINUTES

SMOKED MUSSELS WITH CHESTNUT MUSHROOMS

—— SERVES 4 ——

	METRIC	IMPERIAL	AMERICAN
Extra virgin olive oil	15 ml	1 tbsp	1 tbsp
Butter	15 g	½ oz	1 tbsp
Garlic cloves, crushed	3	3	3
Chestnut mushrooms, quartered	350 g	12 oz	12 oz
Cans of smoked mussels	2 x 40 g	2 x 1½ oz	2 small
Salt and freshly ground black pepper			
Chopped fresh parsley	15 ml	1 tbsp	1 tbsp
Small bunch of fresh chives, snipped	1	1	1
Wholemeal bread, to serve			

① Heat the oil and butter in a large frying pan (skillet) or wok, then add the garlic and fry (sauté) briefly.

② Add the mushrooms and cook, stirring occasionally, until they are tender and the juices are flowing.

③ Stir in the mussels and heat through.

④ Season well with salt and pepper, then stir in the parsley and chives.

⑤ Serve hot with wedges of wholemeal bread.

PREPARATION TIME: 5 MINUTES
COOKING TIME: 10 MINUTES

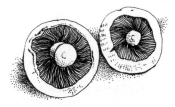

HOT AUBERGINE AND COCONUT STIR-FRY

—— SERVES 4 ——

	METRIC	IMPERIAL	AMERICAN
Large aubergine (eggplant), cut into bite-sized cubes	I	I	I
Salt			
Paprika	5 ml	I tsp	I tsp
Ground fenugreek	2.5 ml	½ tsp	½ tsp
Oil	30 ml	2 tbsp	2 tbsp
Cumin seeds	2.5 ml	½ tsp	½ tsp
Medium onion, finely chopped	I	I	I
Garlic cloves, crushed	2	2	2
Green chillies, seeded and thinly sliced	3	3	3
Ginger purée (paste), from a jar	2.5 ml	½ tsp	½ tsp
Black peppercorns, crushed	2.5 ml	½ tsp	½ tsp
Coconut milk	150 ml	¼ pt	⅔ cup
Chopped fresh coriander (cilantro)	15 ml	I tbsp	I tbsp

①　Place the aubergine in a bowl, sprinkle with salt and leave to stand for about 20 minutes.

②　Rinse the aubergine in cold running water. Pat dry on kitchen paper (paper towels), then toss in the paprika and fenugreek.

③　Heat the oil in a wok or large heavy-based frying pan (skillet) and add the cumin seeds. Fry (sauté) for a few seconds.

④　Add the aubergine, onion, garlic, chillies and ginger and stir-fry until tender.

⑤　Stir in the peppercorns, then the coconut milk. Add salt to taste. Heat through, stirring, but do not allow to boil.

⑥　Serve in individual bowls garnished with the chopped coriander.

PREPARATION TIME: 35 MINUTES
COOKING TIME: 10 MINUTES

TURKEY PURI CHAT

—— SERVES 4 ——

	METRIC	IMPERIAL	AMERICAN
Chapati, paratha and puri mix	½ packet	½ packet	½ packet
Oil for shallow-frying			
Turkey breast, cut into thin strips	225 g	8 oz	8 oz
Onion, thinly sliced	1	1	1
Medium curry paste	30 ml	2 tbsp	2 tbsp
Plain yoghurt	100 ml	3½ fl oz	scant ½ cup
Can of chick peas (garbanzos), drained	200 g	7 oz	1 small
Tamarind chutney	60 ml	4 tbsp	4 tbsp
Chopped fresh coriander (cilantro)	15 ml	1 tbsp	1 tbsp

① Make up the puri mixture according to the packet instructions.

② Roll out the dough to about 5 mm/¼ in thick and cut into about 20 circles using a 6 cm/2½ in cutter.

③ Heat a little oil in a frying pan (skillet) and shallow-fry the puris, a few at a time, until crisp and browned. Drain well, then keep them warm while you fry the remaining puris.

④ Wipe the oil out of the frying pan, add about 15 ml/ 1 tbsp fresh oil and heat.

⑤ Add the turkey and stir-fry until browned on all sides. Stir in the onion and cook until softened.

⑥ Blend in the curry paste and 15 ml/1 tbsp of the yoghurt and cook for a few minutes.

⑦ Stir in the chick peas and heat through.

⑧ Divide the mixture between the puris, spooning on to the top. Spoon a little of the remaining yoghurt on to the middle of the turkey mixture on each puri, then add a little tamarind chutney. Sprinkle the chopped coriander over and serve.

PREPARATION TIME: 25 MINUTES
COOKING TIME: 25 MINUTES

SEAFOOD

Seafood is ideal for the cook with no time to spare. Preparation is often minimal, cooking times are very short, and in many cases all you require is a tasty sauce or a few herbs to make a light and appetising dish. Take advantage of the range of interesting fish available on the wet-fish counter of your local supermarket rather than relying on frozen fish – although that makes a great standby to keep in the freezer.

MEDITERRANEAN SEAFOOD LASAGNE
—— SERVES 4 ——

	METRIC	IMPERIAL	AMERICAN
Passata (sieved tomatoes) with basil	300 ml	½ pt	1¼ cups
Chopped fresh oregano	15 ml	1 tbsp	1 tbsp
Shelled cockles, fresh or thawed frozen	350 g	12 oz	12 oz
Salt and freshly ground black pepper			
Can of creamed mushrooms	400 g	14 oz	1 large
Cooked shelled prawns (shrimp), fresh or thawed frozen	350 g	12 oz	12 oz
Sheets of no-need-to-precook lasagne	9	9	9
Strong Cheddar cheese, grated	75 g	3 oz	¾ cup
Fresh Parmesan, finely grated	25 g	1 oz	¼ cup
Dressed green salad, to serve			

① Make the first sauce by combining the passata, oregano and cockles. Season to taste with salt and pepper.

② Make the second sauce by mixing the creamed mushrooms with the prawns. Season to taste with salt and pepper.

③ Place half the cockle mixture in the bottom of a rectangular lasagne dish and cover with three sheets of lasagne.

④ Place half the prawn mixture on top of this and cover with another three sheets of lasagne.

⑤ Repeat this process with the remaining sauces and top with a layer of grated Cheddar and Parmesan cheese.

⑥ Bake in a preheated oven at 190°C/375°F/gas mark 5 for 30–40 minutes until golden and bubbling.

⑦ Serve with a dressed green salad.

PREPARATION TIME: 15 MINUTES
COOKING TIME: 40 MINUTES

COCKLES IN A MILD MUSTARD SAUCE

—— SERVES 4 ——

	METRIC	IMPERIAL	AMERICAN
Butter or margarine	15 g	½ oz	1 tbsp
Garlic clove, crushed	1	1	1
Large onion, thinly sliced	1	1	1
Shelled cockles, fresh or thawed frozen	700 g	1½ lb	1½ lb
Made English mustard	5 ml	1 tsp	1 tsp
Double (heavy) cream	300 ml	½ pt	1¼ cups
Cornflour (cornstarch)	5 ml	1 tsp	1 tsp
Chopped fresh parsley	15 ml	1 tbsp	1 tbsp
Salt and freshly ground black pepper			
Creamed potatoes and French (green) beans, to serve			

① Heat the butter or margarine in a large pan and add the garlic and onion. Fry (sauté) gently over a moderate heat for about 10 minutes until the onions are very soft.

② Add the cockles and cook for several minutes.

③ Stir in the mustard, then gradually blend in the cream.

④ Mix the cornflour to a paste with a little water, then stir into the cockle mixture. Heat, stirring, until the sauce thickens.

⑤ Add the parsley and season to taste with salt and pepper.

⑥ Serve with creamed potatoes and French beans.

PREPARATION TIME: 5 MINUTES
COOKING TIME: 15 MINUTES

SUPREME CRAB OMELETTE

—— SERVES 1 ——

	METRIC	IMPERIAL	AMERICAN
Oil	15 ml	1 tbsp	1 tbsp
Chopped fresh lemon grass	15 ml	1 tbsp	1 tbsp
Green chilli, seeded and finely chopped	15 ml	1 tbsp	1 tbsp
Garlic clove, crushed	1	1	1
Light soy sauce	15 ml	1 tbsp	1 tbsp
Eggs, lightly beaten	2	2	2
Salt and freshly ground black pepper			
Crab meat, mixed white and brown	100 g	4 oz	4 oz
Fromage frais	15 ml	1 tbsp	1 tbsp
Chopped fresh coriander (cilantro)	10 ml	2 tsp	2 tsp
Green salad, to serve			

① Heat the oil in a medium frying pan (skillet). Add the lemon grass, chilli and garlic and fry (sauté) for about 30 seconds until tender.

② Mix the soy sauce into the beaten eggs, season well, then pour into the frying pan.

③ Cook over a moderate heat, tilting the pan to ensure that the egg mixture runs underneath and cooks on the base of the pan.

④ When the omelette is almost set, combine the crab meat with the fromage frais, season well with salt and pepper, then spoon over the omelette.

⑤ Sprinkle over the coriander, then use a fish slice or spatula to fold the omelette in half and slide it out on to a warm serving plate.

⑥ Serve with a crisp green salad.

PREPARATION TIME: 5 MINUTES
COOKING TIME: 10 MINUTES

SUMMER PRAWNS

—— SERVES 4 ——

	METRIC	IMPERIAL	AMERICAN
Oil	15 ml	1 tbsp	1 tbsp
Garlic clove, crushed	1	1	1
Spring onions (scallions), thinly sliced	6	6	6
Celery sticks, very finely chopped	2	2	2
Shelled frozen prawns (shrimp), thawed	350 g	12 oz	12 oz
Thai fish sauce	15 ml	1 tbsp	1 tbsp
Medium cucumber, peeled, seeded and finely diced	½	½	½
Finely chopped fresh fennel	15 ml	1 tbsp	1 tbsp
Finely chopped fresh parsley	15 ml	1 tbsp	1 tbsp
Salt and freshly ground black pepper			
Crusty bread and a tomato salad, to serve			

① Heat the oil in a wok or large heavy-based frying pan (skillet). Add the garlic, spring onions and celery and stir-fry until the celery is starting to turn transparent.

② Add the prawns and fish sauce and cook for a few minutes to heat through.

③ Stir in the remaining ingredients and cook briefly until hot.

④ Serve hot with fresh crusty bread and a tomato salad.

PREPARATION TIME: 10 MINUTES

COOKING TIME: 5 MINUTES

SEAFOOD AND BROCCOLI SOUFFLÉ
—— SERVES 4 ——

	METRIC	IMPERIAL	AMERICAN
Butter or oil, for greasing			
Leftover mashed potato OR instant mashed potato mixture to make 3 servings			
Butter	15 ml	1 tbsp	1 tbsp
Leftover broccoli, mashed	225 g	8 oz	8 oz
Canned condensed mushroom soup	60 ml	4 tbsp	4 tbsp
Single (light) cream	15 ml	1 tbsp	1 tbsp
Button mushrooms, finely chopped	4	4	4
Cheddar cheese, grated	75 g	3 oz	¾ cup
Parmesan cheese, finely grated	25 g	1 oz	¼ cup
Eggs, separated	3	3	3
Frozen mixed shellfish, thawed	450 g	1 lb	1 lb
Salt and freshly ground black pepper			
Tomato and basil salad, to serve			

1. Grease an 18 cm/7 in soufflé dish with butter or oil.

2. If using instant mash, reconstitute according to the packet directions.

3. Stir the potato, butter, broccoli, soup, cream, mushrooms, cheeses, egg yolks and shellfish into the dish. Season generously with salt and pepper.

4. Whisk the egg whites until stiff, then fold them into the potato mixture with a metal spoon.

5. Spoon into the prepared dish and bake in a preheated oven at 220°C/425°F/gas mark 7 for about 30 minutes until well risen and lightly browned.

6. Serve immediately with a tomato and basil salad.

PREPARATION TIME: 15 MINUTES
COOKING TIME: 30 MINUTES

FILO SALMON PARCELS WITH PRAWNS

—— SERVES 4 ——

	METRIC	IMPERIAL	AMERICAN
Sheets of filo pastry (paste)	6	6	6
Olive oil, for brushing			
Salmon steaks	4	4	4
Cooked shelled prawns (shrimp), fresh or thawed frozen	225 g	8 oz	8 oz
Fromage frais	60 ml	4 tbsp	4 tbsp
Chopped fresh parsley	15 ml	1 tbsp	1 tbsp
Snipped fresh chives	45 ml	3 tbsp	3 tbsp
Finely grated lemon zest	5 ml	1 tsp	1 tsp
Paprika	2.5 ml	½ tsp	½ tsp
Salt and freshly ground black pepper			
Sauté potatoes and French (green) beans, to serve			

① Halve each sheet of pastry across the width. Brush each sheet with olive oil and stack in threes to give four stacks.

② Place a salmon steak in the middle of each stack.

③ Divide the prawns between the four salmon steaks.

④ Combine all the remaining ingredients, seasoning to taste with salt and pepper. Divide the mixture between the four parcels, spooning on top of the prawns.

⑤ Fold the pastry over to enclose the contents, brush the edges of the pastry with oil and seal down.

⑥ Place on a baking (cookie) sheet and cook in a preheated oven at 220°C/425°F/gas mark 7 for 12–15 minutes until crisp and golden.

⑦ Serve with sauté potatoes and French beans.

PREPARATION TIME: 20 MINUTES
COOKING TIME: 15 MINUTES

CHARGRILLED SALMON AND HORSERADISH CREAM
—— SERVES 4 ——

	METRIC	IMPERIAL	AMERICAN
Soured (dairy sour) cream	150 ml	¼ pt	⅔ cup
Creamed horseradish sauce	10 ml	2 tsp	2 tsp
Salt and freshly ground black pepper			
Olive oil, for brushing			
A squeeze of lemon juice			
Small salmon fillets, halved lengthways	4	4	4
English muffins, split	4	4	4
Rocket leaves	32	32	32
Can of lumpfish roe	50 g	2 oz	1 small

① Make the cream by combining the soured cream and horseradish and seasoning to taste with salt and pepper.

② Heat a ribbed griddle on the hob and brush with oil.

③ Squeeze the lemon juice all over the salmon pieces and place on the griddle.

④ Cook until browned on one side, then turn over and cook for a few more minutes on the other side.

⑤ Meanwhile, place the muffin halves on the griddle, cut side down.

⑥ Cook both the salmon and muffin halves until they have brown rib marks.

⑦ Place four rocket leaves, then a piece of salmon on each muffin half. Top this with a dollop of the horseradish cream and then a small spoonful of the lumpfish roe.

⑧ Serve immediately while hot as a light lunch or snack.

PREPARATION TIME: 10 MINUTES
COOKING TIME: 10 MINUTES

CARAMELISED SALMON FILLETS

—— SERVES 4 ——

	METRIC	IMPERIAL	AMERICAN
Mango chutney	45 ml	3 tbsp	3 tbsp
Salmon fillets	4	4	4
Oil	30 ml	2 tbsp	2 tbsp
Finely grated lemon zest	10 ml	2 tsp	2 tsp
Lemon juice	15 ml	1 tbsp	1 tbsp
Small red chillies, seeded and very finely chopped	2	2	2
Extra virgin olive oil	15 ml	1 tbsp	1 tbsp
Syrup from jar of stem ginger OR ginger wine	30 ml	2 tbsp	2 tbsp
Salt			
New potatoes and purple sprouting broccoli, to serve			

① Spread 30 ml/2 tbsp of the mango chutney over both sides of all the salmon fillets.

② In a large frying pan (skillet), heat the oil until very hot, then carefully lay the salmon fillets in the pan, skin side down, and cook for about 3 minutes so that the skin is crisp and the mango chutney has caramelised to a crisp brown coating.

③ Turn the fillets over and cook for a further 2–3 minutes until the second side is also browned and slightly crisp. Remove from the pan and keep warm.

④ Combine the remaining ingredients, adding salt to taste, and pour into the pan. Heat until boiling, stirring constantly.

⑤ Serve the fillets with the spicy glaze poured over them. New potatoes in their skins and purple-sprouting broccoli make excellent accompaniments.

PREPARATION TIME: 5 MINUTES
COOKING TIME: 10 MINUTES

SMOKED SALMON FONDUE
—— SERVES 4 ——

	METRIC	IMPERIAL	AMERICAN
Butter	25 g	1 oz	2 tbsp
Plain (all-purpose) flour	25 g	1 oz	¼ cup
Milk	150 ml	¼ pt	⅔ cup
Wholegrain mustard	15 ml	1 tbsp	1 tbsp
Salt and freshly ground black pepper			
Strong Cheddar cheese, grated	225 g	8 oz	2 cups
Dry white wine	150 ml	¼ pt	⅔ cup
Smoked salmon, cut into fine strips	175 g	6 oz	6 oz
Chopped fresh parsley	15 ml	1 tbsp	1 tbsp
Soured (dairy sour) cream	150 ml	¼ pt	⅔ cup
Bread, crackers and fingers of toast, to serve			

① Heat the butter in a large saucepan or flameproof casserole dish (Dutch oven) and stir in the flour. Cook for a minute or so, stirring continously, then gradually blend in the milk.

② Bring to the boil and cook until smooth and thick, stirring continuously.

③ Stir in the mustard, salt and pepper to taste, cheese and wine and bring back to the boil.

④ Reduce the heat, stir in the salmon, parsley and cream and warm through.

⑤ Serve hot with bread, crackers and fingers of toast for dipping in the fondue.

PREPARATION TIME: 5 MINUTES
COOKING TIME: 10 MINUTES

GLAZED HALIBUT STEAKS
—— SERVES 4 ——

	METRIC	IMPERIAL	AMERICAN
Butter	30 ml	2 tbsp	2 tbsp
Sun-dried tomatoes, finely chopped	25 g	1 oz	1 oz
Bottled chopped shallots with balsamic vinegar	7.5 ml	1½ tsp	1½ tsp
Olive oil	15 ml	1 tbsp	1 tbsp
Small halibut steaks	4	4	4
New potatoes and seasonal baby vegetables, to serve			

① Make the tomato butter by mashing together the butter, tomatoes and shallots. Pile on to a piece of clingfilm (plastic wrap) and shape into a rough sausage. Wrap in clingfilm and place in the refrigerator for about 30 minutes to harden.

② Preheat the oven to 190°C/375°F/gas mark 5.

③ Pour the oil into an ovenproof dish and place in the oven for a few minutes to heat.

④ Place the halibut in the dish and return to the oven. Cook for 10–20 minutes, depending on the thickness of the steaks.

⑤ Meanwhile, slice the tomato butter into eight equal-sized medallions.

⑥ Remove the fish from the oven and, while still very hot, place two medallions of butter on each halibut steak so that it just starts to melt.

⑦ Serve with new potatoes and seasonal baby vegetables.

PREPARATION TIME: 5 MINUTES PLUS CHILLING TIME
COOKING TIME: 20 MINUTES

PARMESAN ROAST COD WITH FENNEL AND LEEKS
—— SERVES 4 ——

	METRIC	IMPERIAL	AMERICAN
Extra virgin olive oil	30 ml	2 tbsp	2 tbsp
Fennel bulb, thinly sliced	1	1	1
Large leek, thinly sliced	1	1	1
Garlic cloves, thinly sliced	5	5	5
Coarse salt			
Freshly ground black pepper			
Thick pieces of cod fillet, about 200 g/7 oz each	4	4	4
Very finely grated fresh Parmesan cheese	90 ml	6 tbsp	6 tbsp
Jacket potatoes and mixed salad, to serve			

① Place the oil, fennel, leek, garlic and salt and pepper in a roasting tin (pan) and mix together so that the vegetables are coated in the oil.

② Cook in a preheated oven at 200°C/400°F/gas mark 6 for about 15 minutes.

③ Meanwhile, coat the cod in the grated Parmesan cheese.

④ Remove the roasting tin from the oven and stir the vegetables. Lay the coated cod pieces on top and sprinkle any remaining Parmesan over the vegetables.

⑤ Return to the oven and cook for 15 minutes so that the vegetables are tender and browned and the fish is starting to flake.

⑥ Serve with jacket potatoes and a simple mixed salad.

PREPARATION TIME: 15 MINUTES
COOKING TIME: 30 MINUTES

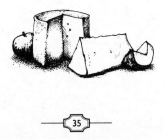

TUNA IN PEPPER AND GARLIC SAUCE

—— SERVES 2 ——

	METRIC	IMPERIAL	AMERICAN
Oil	15 ml	1 tbsp	1 tbsp
Small onion, chopped	1	1	1
Garlic clove, crushed	1	1	1
Small red (bell) pepper, seeded and thinly sliced	½	½	½
Mushrooms, sliced	50 g	2 oz	2 oz
Plain (all-purpose) flour	15 ml	1 tbsp	1 tbsp
Milk	150 ml	¼ pt	⅔ cup
Can of tuna in brine, drained	185 g	6½ oz	1 small
Strong Cheddar cheese, grated	75 g	3 oz	¾ cup
Salt and freshly ground black pepper			
Freshly cooked tagliatelle, to serve			

① Heat the oil in a saucepan, add the onion, then the garlic and pepper slices and cook until softened.

② Add the mushrooms and cook for a few more minutes.

③ Sprinkle the flour over and stir well.

④ Gradually stir in the milk and cook until thickened.

⑤ Stir in the tuna, then the cheese and heat through. Season well with salt and pepper.

⑥ Serve hot with the tagliatelle.

PREPARATION TIME: 10 MINUTES
COOKING TIME: 10 MINUTES

GOAN COD

—— SERVES 4 ——

	METRIC	IMPERIAL	AMERICAN
Cod fillet	450 g	1 lb	1 lb
Vinegar	10 ml	2 tsp	2 tsp
Garlic clove	1	1	1
Shallots, halved	2	2	2
Ground almonds	50 g	2 oz	½ cup
Can of chopped tomatoes	410 g	14½ oz	1 large
Korma curry paste	15 ml	1 tbsp	1 tbsp
Plain yoghurt	150 ml	¼ pt	⅔ cup
Salt and freshly ground black pepper			
Flaked (slivered) almonds	25 g	1 oz	¼ cup
Sultanas (golden raisins)	25 g	1 oz	⅙ cup
Pilau rice or warm crusty bread, to serve.			

① Place the fish in a fairly deep ovenproof dish and sprinkle with the vinegar. Put in a preheated oven at 190°C/375°F/gas mark 5 for 5–10 minutes to evaporate the vinegar.

② Meanwhile, place the garlic, shallots, ground almonds, tomatoes, curry paste, yoghurt and seasoning in a liquidiser or processor and work to a smooth consistency.

③ Pour over the fish, cover well with a lid or foil and return to the oven for about 30 minutes.

④ Sprinkle the almonds and sultanas over the fish and return, uncovered, to the oven for another 10 minutes.

⑤ Serve with pilau rice or warm crusty bread.

PREPARATION TIME: 5 MINUTES
COOKING TIME: 50 MINUTES

BAKED FAT BASS
—— SERVES 4 ——

	METRIC	IMPERIAL	AMERICAN
Whole sea bass, about 1.75 kg/4 lb	1	1	1
Fresh white breadcrumbs	50 g	2 oz	1 cup
Milk	45 ml	3 tbsp	3 tbsp
Spring onions (scallions), finely chopped	4	4	4
Garlic cloves, crushed	2	2	2
Ginger purée (paste), from a jar	5 ml	1 tsp	1 tsp
Thai fish sauce	10 ml	2 tsp	2 tsp
Cashew nuts, halved	25 g	1 oz	¼ cup
Freshly ground black pepper			
Butter, softened	50 g	2 oz	½ cup
Finely shredded lemon grass	15 ml	1 tbsp	1 tbsp
New potatoes and Quick Garlic and Mushroom Spinach (see page 91), to serve			

① To prepare the fish, cut off the fins and gills, then turn the fish over and cut through the backbone at the head and tail. Carefully lift out the backbone. Check for any other bones and remove them.

② Combine the breadcrumbs with the milk, then squeeze out any excess liquid. Mix the breadcrumbs with the spring onions, garlic, ginger, Thai fish sauce and cashew nuts. Add pepper to taste.

③ Lay the fish on the middle of a large sheet of greaseproof (waxed) paper and spoon the breadcrumb mixture into the cavity. Secure with cocktail sticks (toothpicks) or skewers.

④ Combine the butter with the lemon grass and spread over the surface of the fish.

⑤   Fold up the paper around the fish to enclose it, rolling the edges tightly to secure it. Place the parcel on a baking (cookie) sheet and cook in a preheated oven at 180°C/325°F/gas mark 4 for 30–40 minutes until the fish flakes easily when tested with a fork.

⑥   Remove the cocktail sticks (toothpicks) or skewers and serve the fish directly from the parcel accompanied by new potatoes and Quick Garlic and Mushroom Spinach.

PREPARATION TIME: 20 MINUTES

COOKING TIME: 40 MINUTES

SEAFOOD IN A PIMIENTO CREAM SAUCE

—— SERVES 4 ——

	METRIC	IMPERIAL	AMERICAN
Extra virgin olive oil	10 ml	2 tsp	2 tsp
Small red onion, finely chopped	1	1	1
Garlic purée (paste)	10 ml	2 tsp	2 tsp
Mixed frozen shellfish, thawed	400 g	14 oz	14 oz
Tub of sweet pepper pasta sauce	150 g	5 oz	1 small
Whipping cream	75 ml	5 tbsp	5 tbsp
Salt and freshly ground black pepper			
Green salad and crusty bread, to serve			

①   Heat the oil in a large frying pan (skillet), add the onion and garlic purée and fry (sauté) until lightly browned.

②   Add the shellfish and fry, stirring, for about 5 minutes.

③   Stir in the pepper sauce and heat through, then blend in the cream, season to taste with salt and pepper and simmer briefly.

④   Serve with a crisp green salad and warm crusty bread.

PREPARATION TIME: 5 MINUTES

COOKING TIME: 10 MINUTES

GRILLED PLAICE FILLETS WITH LIME AND GINGER
—— SERVES 4 ——

	METRIC	IMPERIAL	AMERICAN
Plaice fillets	700 g	1½ lb	1½ lb
Lime juice	60 ml	4 tbsp	4 tbsp
Very finely chopped fresh root ginger	15 ml	1 tbsp	1 tbsp
Extra virgin olive oil	15 ml	1 tbsp	1 tbsp
Thai fish sauce	10 ml	2 tsp	2 tsp
Spring onions (scallions), finely shredded	3	3	3
Creamed potatoes and mangetout (snow peas), to serve			

① Preheat the grill (broiler) to a moderate heat and line the grill pan with kitchen foil. Arrange the fish in the grill pan.

② Combine the lime juice, ginger, oil and Thai fish sauce and brush liberally over the fish.

③ Place under the grill and cook for 5–10 minutes.

④ Turn the fish over and pour the remaining dressing all over the fillets.

⑤ Grill (broil) for a further 5 minutes until cooked through, then sprinkle with the spring onion.

⑥ Serve with creamed potatoes and mangetout.

PREPARATION TIME: 5 MINUTES
COOKING TIME: 15 MINUTES

MICROWAVE MACKEREL WITH KIWI FRUIT
—— SERVES 4 ——

	METRIC	IMPERIAL	AMERICAN
Kiwi fruit	3	3	3
Eating (dessert) apple, peeled and grated	I	I	I
Lemon juice	15 ml	I tbsp	I tbsp
Extra virgin olive oil	10 ml	2 tsp	2 tsp
Green peppercorns, roughly crushed	10 ml	2 tsp	2 tsp
Porridge oats	25 g	I oz	¼ cup
Fresh wholemeal breadcrumbs	25 g	I oz	½ cup
Chopped fresh thyme	5 ml	I tsp	I tsp
Chopped fresh lemon balm (optional)	5 ml	I tsp	I tsp
Coarse salt			
Mackerel, cleaned	4	4	4
Ciabatta bread and green salad, to serve			

① Peel the kiwi fruit. Slice one and reserve for garnish.

② Finely chop the other two and place in a bowl with all the other ingredients except the mackerel, adding salt to taste.

③ Spoon the mixture into the cavity of each mackerel and secure using cocktail sticks (toothpicks).

④ Place the stuffed fish in a shallow microwave proof dish. Microwave on High (650w) for 4–6 minutes until the fish flakes easily when tested with a fork. Adjust the timing if you have a more or less powerful microwave.

⑤ Garnish with the reserved slices of kiwi fruit and serve with warm ciabatta bread and a crisp green salad.

PREPARATION TIME: 10 MINUTES
COOKING TIME: 6 MINUTES

SNAPPER WITH FRESH HERBS IN PROSCIUTTO

—— SERVES 4 ——

	METRIC	IMPERIAL	AMERICAN
Sprigs of fresh thyme	4	4	4
Sprigs of fresh rosemary	4	4	4
Chopped fresh dill (dill weed)	20 ml	4 tsp	4 tsp
Whole small red snapper, cleaned and scaled	4	4	4
Long slices of prosciutto or cured ham	8	8	8
Lemon-flavoured olive oil	45 ml	3 tbsp	3 tbsp
Garlic clove, crushed	I	I	I
Chopped fresh thyme	20 ml	4 tsp	4 tsp
Freshly ground black pepper			
Coarse salt			
Potato salad and sliced beef tomatoes, to serve			

① Divide the sprigs of thyme and rosemary and the chopped dill between the cavities of each fish.

② Lay out four squares of greaseproof (waxed) paper, each large enough to enclose a fish, and place two slices of prosciutto side by side in the centre of each one. Place a fish on top of the two pieces of prosciutto and wrap the prosciutto neatly around.

③ Combine the oil with the garlic, chopped thyme and seasoning and drizzle over the fish.

④ Fold up the squares of paper round the fish and seal in carefully by rolling the edges tightly.

⑤ Place the four parcels on a baking (cookie) sheet and cook in a preheated oven at 180°C/350°F/gas mark 4 for about 20–25 minutes until the fish flakes easily when tested with a fork.

⑥ Serve with a potato salad and sliced beef tomatoes.

PREPARATION TIME: 15 MINUTES
COOKING TIME: 25 MINUTES

CREAMY COCONUT FISH AND MUSHROOM RISOTTO

—— SERVES 4 ——

	METRIC	IMPERIAL	AMERICAN
Extra virgin olive oil	30 ml	2 tbsp	2 tbsp
Cumin seeds	2.5 ml	½ tsp	½ tsp
Fennel seeds	2.5 ml	½ tsp	½ tsp
Black mustard seeds	7.5 ml	1½ tsp	1½ tsp
Garlic cloves, crushed	2	2	2
Large red onions, chopped	2	2	2
Arborio rice	350 g	12 oz	1½ cups
Fish stock (bouillon) cube	1	1	1
Boiling water	600 ml	1 pt	2½ cups
Wholegrain mustard	15 ml	1 tbsp	1 tbsp
Wild mushrooms, cut into bite-sized pieces	175 g	6 oz	6 oz
Huss, boned and cut into chunks	350 g	12 oz	12 oz
Coconut milk	300 ml	½ pt	1¼ cups
Salt and freshly ground black pepper			
Poppy seeds and toasted sesame seeds, to garnish			

① Heat the oil in a large pan, add the cumin, fennel and mustard seeds and fry (sauté) for a few seconds.

② Add the garlic and onions and fry until golden.

③ Add the rice and cook until the grains are coated in oil, stirring constantly.

④ Crumble in the stock cube and stir in the boiling water. Cook for about 10 minutes until most of the liquid has been absorbed.

⑤ Stir in the mustard and mushrooms and cook for about 2 minutes.

⑥ Add the huss and coconut milk and simmer for a further 5–10 minutes until most of the liquid has been absorbed. Season to taste with salt and pepper.

⑦ Serve hot garnished with poppy and sesame seeds.

PREPARATION TIME: 15 MINUTES
COOKING TIME: 35 MINUTES

WHITING WITH SMOKED BACON IN CIDER

—— SERVES 4 ——

	METRIC	IMPERIAL	AMERICAN
Bacon lardons	75 g	3 oz	3 oz
Small shallots	100 g	4 oz	4 oz
Whiting fillets, about 175 g/6 oz each, skinned	4	4	4
Dried chervil	2.5 ml	½ tsp	½ tsp
Chopped fresh parsley	10 ml	2 tsp	2 tsp
Dry cider	150 ml	¼ pt	⅔ cup
Fish stock	90 ml	6 tbsp	6 tbsp
Salt and freshly ground black pepper			
Crème fraîche	60 ml	4 tbsp	4 tbsp
Sprigs of fresh parsley, to garnish			
New potatoes and steamed asparagus, to serve			

① Briskly fry (sauté) the bacon lardons in a flameproof casserole dish (Dutch oven) until the fat runs.

② Add the shallots and continue to cook until they have started to soften.

③ Lay the whiting fillets in the casserole, sprinkle the chervil and chopped parsley over and pour on the cider and stock. Season to taste with salt and pepper. Cover tightly with kitchen foil and cook in a preheated oven at 190°C/375°F/gas mark 5 for about 20 minutes until the fish flakes when tested with a fork.

④ Carefully lift out the fish and keep warm.

⑤ Place the casserole back on the heat and boil for a few minutes to reduce the liquid a little.

⑥ Reduce the heat, stir in the crème fraîche and heat through gently without allowing the sauce to boil.

⑦ Serve the fish surrounded by a pool of the sauce, garnished with sprigs of fresh parsley and accompanied by new potatoes and steamed fresh asparagus.

PREPARATION TIME: 5 MINUTES
COOKING TIME: 40 MINUTES

GRILLED TROUT WITH TARRAGON

—— SERVES 4 ——

	METRIC	IMPERIAL	AMERICAN
Cleaned trout, about 350 g/12 oz each	4	4	4
Butter, melted	25 g	1 oz	2 tbsp
Chopped fresh tarragon	15 ml	1 tbsp	1 tbsp
For the dressing:			
Soured (dairy sour) cream	150 ml	¼ pt	⅔ cup
Cayenne	1.5 ml	¼ tsp	¼ tsp
Toasted flaked (slivered) almonds	75 g	3 oz	¾ cup
Salt and freshly ground black pepper			
Finely chopped fresh tarragon	5 ml	1 tsp	1 tsp
Sauté potatoes and mixed salad, to serve			

① Brush the trout with the melted butter and place the tarragon in the cavities of the fish.

② Grill (broil) the fish under a preheated medium grill (broiler) for a few minutes on each side until cooked to the bone.

③ Combine all the dressing ingredients, seasoning to taste with salt and pepper.

④ Lay the fish on individual plates and place a spoonful of the dressing beside each. Serve with sauté potatoes and a mixed salad.

PREPARATION TIME: 10 MINUTES
COOKING TIME: 10 MINUTES

MEAT

A one-pan meat dish doesn't have to be a casserole, as you might expect. In this section, I show you how you can create delicious main courses to be cooked in the oven, on the hob or under the grill (broiler), with a variety of crusts and toppings, sauces and dressings – all in one dish. Remember that the cheaper the cut, the better it will react to longer cooking, while quick-cooking recipes call for better cuts of meat.

MINTED LAMB AND APPLE CASSEROLE
—— SERVES 4 ——

	METRIC	IMPERIAL	AMERICAN
Plain (all-purpose) flour	50 g	2 oz	½ cup
Salt and freshly ground black pepper			
Stewing lamb, diced	700 g	1½ lb	1½ lb
Oil	30 ml	2 tbsp	2 tbsp
Large leek, thinly sliced	1	1	1
Large eating (dessert) apples, peeled, cored and thickly sliced	3	3	3
Dry white wine	150 ml	¼ pt	⅔ cup
Chicken or vegetable stock	450 ml	¾ pt	2 cups
Chopped fresh mint	60 ml	4 tbsp	4 tbsp
Sugar	5 ml	1 tsp	1 tsp
Frozen peas	100 g	4 oz	4 oz
Sprigs of mint	4	4	4
Creamed potatoes and baby carrots, to serve			

1. Season the flour with salt and pepper, then toss the lamb in the flour, shaking off any excess.

2. Heat the oil in a flameproof casserole dish (Dutch oven), then add the lamb and fry (sauté) briefly until browned on all sides.

3. Stir in the leek and apple, then sprinkle on any remaining seasoned flour and stir in the wine and stock. Add the chopped mint and sugar, season with salt and pepper, then cover well and cook in a preheated oven at 180°C/350°C/gas mark 4 for about 1¼ hours.

4. Add the frozen peas to the casserole, cover and return to the oven for a further 15–30 minutes or until the meat is very tender.

5. Garnish with sprigs of mint and serve accompanied by creamed potatoes and baby carrots.

PREPARATION TIME: 15 MINUTES
COOKING TIME: 2½ HOURS

JERK LAMB WITH CORNBREAD TOPPING
—— SERVES 4 ——

	METRIC	IMPERIAL	AMERICAN
Lean lamb, cut into small cubes	450 g	1 lb	1 lb
For the marinade:			
Jerk seasoning	10 ml	2 tsp	2 tsp
Lemon juice	30 ml	2 tbsp	2 tbsp
Muscovado sugar	5 ml	1 tsp	1 tsp
Garlic clove, crushed	1	1	1
For the lamb layer:			
Oil	30 ml	2 tbsp	2 tbsp
Garlic cloves, crushed	2	2	2
Garlic cloves, cut into fine slivers	4	4	4
Green chillies, seeded and cut into fine strips	3	3	3
Shallots, halved	8	8	8
Red (bell) pepper, seeded and cut into eight	1	1	1
Yellow pepper, seeded and cut into eight	1	1	1
Jerk seasoning	5 ml	1 tsp	1 tsp
Sun-dried tomato purée (paste)	45 ml	3 tbsp	3 tbsp
Stock	300 ml	½ pt	1¼ cups
Muscovado sugar	5 ml	1 tsp	1 tsp
Tabasco sauce	2.5 ml	½ tsp	½ tsp
For the cornbread:			
Instant polenta (cornmeal)	175 g	6 oz	1½ cups
Self-raising (self-rising) flour	175 g	6 oz	1½ cups
Caster (superfine) sugar	25 g	1 oz	2 tbsp
Baking powder	10 ml	2 tsp	2 tsp
Salt	5 ml	1 tsp	1 tsp
Chopped fresh thyme	10 ml	2 tsp	2 tsp
Eggs	2	2	2
Milk	250 ml	8 fl oz	1 cup
Butter, melted	50 g	2 oz	¼ cup
Roughly chopped fresh rosemary	10 ml	2 tsp	2 tsp
Tomato, broccoli and basil salad, to serve			

① Combine the marinade ingredients and stir in the lamb. Cover and refrigerate for about 1 hour.

② Heat the oil in a flameproof casserole (Dutch oven) of medium depth and at least 20 cm/8 in in diameter.

③ Add all the garlic, the chillies and shallots and fry (sauté) for about 5 minutes or until soft.

④ Remove the lamb from the marinade, add to the casserole and fry until browned on all sides.

⑤ Stir in any marinade juice and the peppers and cook for a further few minutes, then add the jerk seasoning, tomato purée, stock, sugar and Tabasco sauce.

⑥ Cover and simmer for 20–30 minutes or until the meat is tender.

⑦ To make the cornbread, place the polenta, flour, sugar, baking powder, salt and thyme in a large mixing bowl. Make a well in the middle and add the eggs, milk and melted butter. Beat with a wooden spoon to make a soft batter.

⑧ Remove the lamb mixture from the heat and allow to cool slightly for about 5 minutes.

⑨ Spoon the cornbread batter all over the lamb mixture, ensuring it reaches the edges of the dish. Sprinkle the rosemary all over the surface.

⑩ Cook in a preheated oven at 200°C/400°F/gas mark 6 for about 30 minutes or until the bread is golden and risen and a skewer comes away clean when pushed into the centre.

⑪ Slice into large chunks and serve hot with a tomato, broccoli and basil salad.

PREPARATION TIME: 20 MINUTES PLUS 1 HOUR MARINATING TIME
COOKING TIME: 1 HOUR

LAMB, MUSHROOM AND MADEIRA PUDDING
—— SERVES 4 ——

	METRIC	IMPERIAL	AMERICAN
For the suet crust:			
Self-raising (self-rising) flour	450 g	I lb	4 cups
Shredded (chopped) suet	225 g	8 oz	2 cups
Dried thyme	2.5 ml	½ tsp	½ tsp
Dried rosemary	2.5 ml	½ tsp	½ tsp
Dried parsley	2.5 ml	½ tsp	½ tsp
Salt			
Water	300 ml	½ pt	1¼ cups
For the filling:			
Lean boneless lamb, cut into bite-sized cubes	700 g	1½ lb	1½ lb
Button mushrooms, quartered	225 g	8 oz	8 oz
Large onion, very finely chopped	I	I	I
Plain (all-purpose) flour	30 ml	2 tbsp	2 tbsp
Madeira	60 ml	4 tbsp	4 tbsp
Salt and freshly ground black pepper			
Creamed potatoes and Brussels sprouts, to serve			

① Place the flour, suet, herbs and a pinch of salt in a bowl and bind to a stiff dough with the water. Roll out the dough to a round about 1 cm/½ in thick and cut off a wedge about one-third of the round.

② Use the larger piece to line a 1.5 litre/2½ pt/6 cup basin.

③ Mix together the filling ingredients, seasoning to taste with salt and pepper. Spoon into the lined basin.

④ Shape the remaining dough to form a lid for the basin, dampen the edges and seal it on.

⑤ Cover the basin with pleated kitchen foil and place in a steamer. Pour boiling water around to come two-thirds of the way up the sides. Steam for about 3 hours, topping up with boiling water as necessary.

⑥ Serve hot with creamed potatoes and Brussels sprouts.

PREPARATION TIME: 30 MINUTES

COOKING TIME: 3 HOURS

PEPPERED LAMB CUTLETS WITH PORT
—— SERVES 4 ——

	METRIC	IMPERIAL	AMERICAN
Small lamb cutlets	8	8	8
Green peppercorns, crushed	15–30 ml	1–2 tbsp	1–2 tbsp
Oil	15 ml	1 tbsp	1 tbsp
Port	60 ml	4 tbsp	4 tbsp
Redcurrant jelly (clear conserve)	30 ml	2 tbsp	2 tbsp
Roast potatoes and a selection of roast root vegetables, to serve			

① Wash the lamb and pat dry on kitchen paper (paper towels). Press the crushed peppercorns into both sides of the cutlets.

② Heat the oil in a frying pan (skillet) and cook the cutlets over a moderate heat until browned on both sides and the juices run clear.

③ Remove the cutlets from the pan and keep warm.

④ Pour the port into the hot pan and boil for a few minutes. Stir in the redcurrant jelly and heat through.

⑤ Pour over the cutlets and serve with roast potatoes and a selection of roast root vegetables.

PREPARATION TIME: 5 MINUTES
COOKING TIME: 15 MINUTES

CRUNCHY LEMON LAMB KEBABS
—— SERVES 4 ——

	METRIC	IMPERIAL	AMERICAN
Lemon juice	30 ml	2 tbsp	2 tbsp
Finely grated lemon zest	15 ml	1 tbsp	1 tbsp
Lemon pepper seasoning	5 ml	1 tsp	1 tsp
Chopped fresh coriander (cilantro)	10 ml	2 tsp	2 tsp
Green peppercorns, roughly crushed	15 ml	1 tbsp	1 tbsp
Coarse salt	10 ml	2 tsp	2 tsp
Boneless lean lamb, cut into bite-sized cubes	450 g	1 lb	1 lb
For the dressing:			
Balsamic vinegar	90 ml	6 tbsp	6 tbsp
Medium red onion, minced (ground) or very finely chopped	1	1	1
Red peppercorns, roughly crushed	5 ml	1 tsp	1 tsp
Selection of salads, to serve			

① Place the lemon juice and zest, lemon pepper, coriander, green peppercorns and salt in a bowl and mix well. Put the lamb into the bowl, and, using your hands, press the mixture into the meat. Leave to marinate for about 1 hour.

② Meanwhile, make the dressing by combining the vinegar, onion and red peppercorns.

③ Thread the lamb on to skewers and place under a preheated medium-hot grill (broiler).

④ Cook for 10–15 minutes, turning frequently, until browned on all sides and the juices run clear.

⑤ Drizzle the dressing over the kebabs and serve with a selection of salads.

PREPARATION TIME: 10 MINUTES PLUS 1 HOUR MARINATING TIME
COOKING TIME: 15 MINUTES

STUFFED ROAST SHOULDER OF LAMB

—— SERVES 4 ——

	METRIC	IMPERIAL	AMERICAN
For the stuffing:			
Fresh breadcrumbs	100 g	4 oz	2 cups
Extra virgin olive oil	15 ml	1 tbsp	1 tbsp
Garlic cloves, crushed	2	2	2
Worcestershire sauce	15 ml	1 tbsp	1 tbsp
Olive paste or pâté	15 ml	1 tbsp	1 tbsp
Anchovies, finely chopped	4	4	4
Chestnut mushrooms, very finely chopped	75 g	3 oz	3 oz
Chopped fresh thyme	15 ml	1 tbsp	1 tbsp
Freshly ground black pepper			
Shoulder of lamb, boned	1	1	1
For the rub:			
Extra virgin olive oil	15 ml	1 tbsp	1 tbsp
Coarse salt			
Sprigs of fresh rosemary, to garnish			
Roast potatoes and seasonal vegetables, to serve			

① Combine all the stuffing ingredients, adding pepper to taste.

② Stuff the joint with the mixture, then roll up and secure well with string or skewers. Weigh the joint and work out the cooking time. Place in a roasting tin (pan) and score the skin into diamond shapes. Rub the oil and salt into the skin and place a few sprigs of rosemary on the joint.

③ Cook in a preheated oven at 180°C/350°F/gas mark 4 for about 35 minutes per 450 g/1 lb plus an extra 20 minutes.

④ Remove from the oven and allow to stand for about 10 minutes before carving.

⑤ Serve with roast potatoes and seasonal vegetables.

PREPARATION TIME: 30 MINUTES

COOKING TIME: 35 MINUTES PER 450 G/1 LB PLUS 20 MINUTES

PORK, PIMIENTO AND PISTACHIO TERRINE

—— SERVES 4 ——

	METRIC	IMPERIAL	AMERICAN
Smoked streaky bacon rashers (slices), rinded	150 g	5 oz	5 oz
Minced pork	450 g	I lb	I lb
Garlic cloves, crushed	2	2	2
Ground mace	2.5 ml	½ tsp	½ tsp
Chopped fresh sage	10 ml	2 tsp	2 tsp
Chopped fresh thyme	5 ml	I tsp	I tsp
Salt and freshly ground black pepper			
Pistachio nuts, shelled and coarsely chopped	100 g	4 oz	I cup
Can of red pimientos, drained and roughly chopped	400 g	14 oz	I large
Watercress and potato salad, to serve			

① Stretch each bacon rasher with the back of a knife to lengthen. Use one-third of the rashers to line a 600 ml/ 1 pt/2½ cup loaf tin (pan).

② Combine the pork with the garlic, mace, sage, thyme, salt and plenty of pepper and mix well.

③ Spoon half the pork mixture into the tin to give an even layer. Sprinkle over half the nuts, then make a layer using half the chopped pimientos. Lay on another third of the bacon. Repeat the layers, finishing with a layer of bacon.

④ Cover with foil, then place in a roasting tin and pour in boiling water to come half way up the sides of the tin.

⑤ Place in a preheated oven at 160°C/325°F/gas mark 3 and cook for 1–1½ hours until the mixture is set and the meat no longer pink.

⑥ Allow to cool a little, then place a weight on top and chill for at least 4 hours.

⑦ Cut into thick slices and serve with watercress and a potato salad.

PREPARATION TIME: 25 MINUTES PLUS 4 HOURS CHILLING TIME
COOKING TIME: 1½ HOURS

BAKED MEDITERRANEAN ROLY POLY

—— SERVES 4 ——

	METRIC	IMPERIAL	AMERICAN
Large red onion, finely chopped	1	1	1
Garlic cloves, finely chopped	3	3	3
Medium red (bell) pepper, seeded and finely chopped	½	½	½
Medium yellow pepper, seeded and finely chopped	½	½	½
Smoked streaky bacon rashers (slices), finely chopped	225 g	8 oz	8 oz
Chopped fresh oregano or marjoram	15 ml	1 tbsp	1 tbsp
Salt and freshly ground black pepper			
Self-raising (self-rising) flour	350 g	12 oz	3 cups
Shredded (chopped) vegetable suet	175 g	6 oz	1½ cups
Sun-dried tomato purée (paste)	30 ml	2 tbsp	2 tbsp
Tomato and basil salad, to serve			

① Combine the onion, garlic, peppers, bacon, herbs and seasoning in a bowl and mix well.

② Mix together the flour and suet, then add enough cold water to make a soft but not sticky dough.

③ Place on a floured board and knead lightly, then roll out to a 30 cm/12 in square.

④ Spread the sun-dried tomato purée over the dough, leaving a 2.5 cm/1 in margin all round. Spread the bacon mixture over the tomato.

⑤ Dampen the edges with water, then roll up. Pinch all the edges to seal, then place on a sheet of kitchen foil and wrap loosely.

⑥ Place on a baking (cookie) sheet and bake in a preheated oven at 200°C/400°F/gas mark 6 for about 1¼ hours until golden brown.

⑦ Serve with a fresh tomato and basil salad.

PREPARATION TIME: 25 MINUTES
COOKING TIME: 1½ HOURS

SOMERSET HAM

—— SERVES 4 ——

	METRIC	IMPERIAL	AMERICAN
Butter	50 g	2 oz	¼ cup
Potatoes, peeled and thinly sliced	450 g	1 lb	1 lb
Cooked ham, cut into small slices	350 g	12 oz	3 cups
Medium onions, sliced	2	2	2
Large eating (dessert) apples, peeled and sliced	2	2	2
Salt and freshly ground black pepper			
Chopped fresh parsley	30 ml	2 tbsp	2 tbsp
Cider	150 ml	¼ pt	⅔ cup
Chicken or ham stock	150 ml	¼ pt	⅔ cup
Milk	300 ml	½ pt	1¼ cups
Peas or runner beans, to serve			

① Rub half the butter around the inside of a large casserole dish (Dutch oven).

② Place about one-third of the potatoes in the bottom of the dish. Cover with half the ham. Use half the onion to make the next layer, then cover with half the apple. Season well with salt and pepper, then sprinkle the parsley over. Repeat the layers, then top with the remaining potatoes.

③ Combine the cider, stock and milk and pour gently into the casserole, allowing it to seep down through the layers.

④ Season the top layer with salt and pepper, then dot with the remaining butter.

⑤ Cover the casserole and cook in a preheated oven at 180°C/350°F/gas mark 4 for 30 minutes.

⑥ Uncover and cook for a further 15 minutes until browned and the potato is soft.

⑦ Serve hot with fresh peas or runner beans.

PREPARATION TIME: 25 MINUTES

COOKING TIME: 45 MINUTES

GAMMON STEAKS IN A PEAR AND GINGER GLAZE

—— SERVES 4 ——

	METRIC	IMPERIAL	AMERICAN
Oil	15 ml	1 tbsp	1 tbsp
Gammon steaks	4	4	4
Canned pear halves, drained and finely chopped	4	4	4
Stem ginger, very finely chopped	25 g	1 oz	1 oz
Syrup from the jar of stem ginger	90 ml	6 tbsp	6 tbsp
Freshly ground black pepper			
New potatoes and runner beans, to serve			

① Heat the oil in a large frying pan (skillet) and fry (sauté) the gammon steaks for about 8 minutes, turning once.

② Add the pear, ginger and syrup and black pepper to taste. Heat through and serve with new potatoes and runner beans.

PREPARATION TIME: 5 MINUTES
COOKING TIME: 10 MINUTES

ZYWIESKA TOMATO BAKE WITH CIABATTA CRUST

—— SERVES 4 ——

	METRIC	IMPERIAL	AMERICAN
Extra virgin olive oil	15 ml	1 tbsp	1 tbsp
Garlic cloves, crushed	3	3	3
Red onions, quartered	3	3	3
Medium red (bell) pepper, seeded and cut into thick slices	1	1	1
Courgettes (zucchini), cut into thick slices	2	2	2
Zywieska sausage, cut into thick slices	350 g	12 oz	12 oz
Passata (sieved tomatoes) with basil	300 ml	½ pt	1¼ cups
Vegetable stock	150 ml	¼ pt	⅔ cup
Can of artichoke hearts, drained	400 g	14 oz	1 large
Stoned (pitted) black olives	12	12	12
Chopped fresh thyme	15 ml	1 tbsp	1 tbsp
Chopped fresh rosemary	15 ml	1 tbsp	1 tbsp
Salt and freshly ground black pepper			
For the crust:			
Butter, softened	50 g	2 oz	¼ cup
Garlic clove, crushed	1	1	1
Chopped fresh thyme	15 ml	1 tbsp	1 tbsp
Chopped fresh rosemary	15 ml	1 tbsp	1 tbsp
Chopped fresh oregano	15 ml	1 tbsp	1 tbsp
Chopped fresh parsley	15 ml	1 tbsp	1 tbsp
Coarse salt and freshly ground black pepper			
Ciabatta loaf, cut into 5 mm/½ in slices	1	1	1
Mixed salad and French dressing, to serve			

① Heat the oil in a flameproof casserole (Dutch oven), add the garlic and onions and fry (sauté) until tender.

② Add the red pepper and courgettes and cook for a further 5 minutes.

③ Stir in the sausage, passata, stock, artichoke hearts, olives and herbs and season to taste with salt and pepper. Simmer for about 5 minutes.

④ Meanwhile, make the crust by combining the butter, garlic, herbs and pepper and salt to taste. Spread over one side of each slice of ciabatta.

⑤ Remove the casserole from the heat and arrange the slices of bread over the surface of the sausage mixture, buttered-side up.

⑥ Place in a preheated oven at 190°C/375°F/gas mark 5 and cook for 20–30 minutes until the crust is golden.

⑦ Serve hot with a mixed salad and French dressing.

PREPARATION TIME: 20 MINUTES
COOKING TIME: 45 MINUTES

PORK PARCELS WITH SMOKED GARLIC
—— SERVES 4 ——

	METRIC	IMPERIAL	AMERICAN
Medium pork chops, trimmed of fat and rind	4	4	4
Smoked garlic cloves, crushed	4	4	4
Smoked garlic cloves, cut into fine slivers	6	6	6
Medium red onion, minced (ground) or very finely chopped	1	1	1
Crème fraîche	150 ml	¼ pt	⅔ cup
Vegetable stock, cool	120 ml	4 fl oz	½ cup
Snipped fresh chives	60 ml	4 tbsp	4 tbsp
Salt and freshly ground black pepper			
New potatoes and mangetout (snow peas), to serve			

① Place each chop in the middle of a large sheet of kitchen foil.

② Combine the remaining ingredients, seasoning to taste with salt and pepper. Divide the mixture between the four chops, spooning it on to the surface of the meat.

③ Pull the foil up around the chops, then seal well by rolling the edges of the foil together.

④ Place in a small ovenproof dish and cook in a preheated oven at 180°C/350°F/gas mark 4 for about 1 hour until tender and the juices of the pork run clear.

⑤ Place each parcel on a plate and open carefully. Serve with new potatoes and mangetout (snow peas).

PREPARATION TIME: 10 MINUTES
COOKING TIME: 1 HOUR

LOIN CHOPS WITH CITRUS TARRAGON BUTTER

—— SERVES 4 ——

	METRIC	IMPERIAL	AMERICAN
Extra virgin olive oil	15 ml	1 tbsp	1 tbsp
Lemon juice	15 ml	1 tbsp	1 tbsp
Freshly ground black pepper			
Pork loin chops	4	4	4
For the Citrus Tarragon Butter:			
Butter, softened	100 g	4 oz	½ cup
Fresh chopped tarragon	5 ml	1 tsp	1 tsp
Finely grated lemon zest	2.5 ml	½ tsp	½ tsp
Finely grated lime zest	2.5 ml	½ tsp	½ tsp
Finely grated orange zest	2.5 ml	½ tsp	½ tsp
Lime juice	5 ml	1 tsp	1 tsp
Coarse salt and freshly ground black pepper			
New potatoes and runner beans, to serve			

① Combine the olive oil, lemon juice and black pepper and brush over one side of the chops. Place them under a preheated grill (broiler) and cook for about 5–10 minutes, depending on their thickness.

② Turn the chops, brush the other side with the mixture and grill for a further 5–10 minutes until cooked and the juices run clear.

③ Meanwhile, combine all the ingredients for the Citrus Tarragon Butter, seasoning to taste with salt and pepper. Form into a small log by rolling in a piece of clingfilm (plastic wrap) and cut into four thick slices.

④ Place a slice of butter on the top of each cooked chop and flash them very briefly under the grill so that the butter just starts to melt.

⑤ Serve with new potatoes and runner beans.

PREPARATION TIME: 15 MINUTES
COOKING TIME: 20 MINUTES

COUSCOUS WITH SALAMI, HERBS AND BRIE

—— SERVES 4 ——

	METRIC	IMPERIAL	AMERICAN
Olive oil	5 ml	I tsp	I tsp
Water	275 ml	9 fl oz	1¼ cups
Salt			
Couscous	250 g	9 oz	1½ cups
Salami, diced	75 g	3 oz	3 oz
Small leek, finely shredded	I	I	I
Garlic cloves, crushed	2	2	2
Medium red (bell) pepper, seeded and finely diced	½	½	½
Roughly chopped fresh mint	30 ml	2 tbsp	2 tbsp
Roughly chopped fresh oregano	30 ml	2 tbsp	2 tbsp
Roughly chopped fresh thyme	15 ml	I tbsp	I tbsp
Brie, diced	75 g	3 oz	¾ cup
Extra virgin olive oil	30 ml	2 tbsp	2 tbsp
Freshly ground black pepper			
Hot garlic bread, to serve			

① Place the olive oil, water and salt in a saucepan and bring to a simmer.

② Stir in the couscous, cover the pan and remove from the heat. Leave to stand for about 3 minutes.

③ Stir in all the remaining ingredients, adding pepper to taste, and return the pan to the heat for a few minutes, stirring well.

④ Fluff up the mixture with a fork.

⑤ Serve warm or cold with hot crusty garlic bread.

PREPARATION TIME: 10 MINUTES
COOKING TIME: 6 MINUTES

CAJUN PORK WITH PEAS

—— SERVES 4 ——

	METRIC	IMPERIAL	AMERICAN
Cajun seasoning	20 ml	4 tsp	4 tsp
Boneless lean pork, thinly sliced	350 g	12 oz	12 oz
Cooked potatoes, diced	3	3	3
Olive oil	15 ml	1 tbsp	1 tbsp
Onions, thinly sliced	2	2	2
Garlic cloves, crushed	2	2	2
Small red (bell) pepper, seeded and diced	1	1	1
Frozen peas	75 g	3 oz	3 oz
Lemon juice	30 ml	2 tbsp	2 tbsp
Green salad and crusty bread, to serve			

① Sprinkle 15 ml/3 tsp of the Cajun seasoning over the pork. Mix well, cover and leave for about 30 minutes.

② Combine the remaining Cajun seasoning with the potatoes.

③ Heat the oil in a wok or large frying pan (skillet), add the onions and garlic and fry (sauté) until well browned.

④ Add the pork and stir-fry for about 10 minutes so that the meat is thoroughly cooked and brown.

⑤ Stir in the red pepper and peas and cook for a further 5 minutes.

⑥ Add the lemon juice, stir and serve hot with a crisp green salad and crusty bread.

PREPARATION TIME: 10 MINUTES PLUS 30 MINUTES MARINATING TIME
COOKING TIME: 20 MINUTES

ST STEPHEN'S BEEF

—— SERVES 4 ——

	METRIC	IMPERIAL	AMERICAN
Stewing beef, cubed	450 g	1 lb	1 lb
Seasoned plain (all-purpose) flour	25 g	1 oz	¼ cup
Oil	30 ml	2 tbsp	2 tbsp
Small shallots	100 g	4 oz	4 oz
Garlic cloves, crushed	2	2	2
Red wine	300 ml	½ pt	1¼ cups
Beef stock	300 ml	½ pt	1¼ cups
Tomato purée (paste)	15 ml	1 tbsp	1 tbsp
Dark brown sugar	15 ml	1 tbsp	1 tbsp
Small button mushrooms, halved	100 g	4 oz	4 oz
Bay leaves	2	2	2
Sprigs of thyme	2	2	2
Pork sausage meat	225 g	8 oz	8 oz
Salt and freshly ground black pepper			
Ground mace	2.5 ml	½ tsp	½ tsp
A little flour, for shaping			
Roast potatoes and a selection of vegetables, to serve			

① Toss the beef in the seasoned flour.

② Heat the oil in a flameproof casserole dish (Dutch oven) and fry (sauté) a few pieces at a time until browned on all sides.

③ Add the shallots and garlic to the pan and cook for a further 3 minutes.

④ Sprinkle any remaining flour into the pan and stir well, scraping up the residue from the bottom of the pan. Gradually add some of the red wine, stirring until the pan is clean and the wine slightly thickened.

⑤ Add the remaining wine, the stock, tomato purée, sugar, mushrooms and herbs to the pan. Stir, cover tightly and cook in a preheated oven at 180°C/350°F/gas mark 4 for about 1 hour.

⑥ Combine the sausage meat with the salt, pepper, and mace. Using floured hands, shape it into balls about the size of a walnut.

⑦ Stir the sausage balls into the casserole, re-cover and continue to cook for a further 1–1½ hours or until the beef is very tender.

⑧ Serve with roast potatoes and a selection of fresh vegetables.

PREPARATION TIME: 20 MINUTES
COOKING TIME: 2–3 HOURS

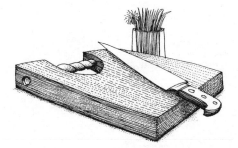

BRAISED BEAUJOLAIS BEEF AND BEANS
—— SERVES 4 ——

	METRIC	IMPERIAL	AMERICAN
Stewing or braising beef	700 g	1½ lb	1½ lb
Seasoned plain (all-purpose) flour	15 ml	1 tbsp	1 tbsp
Oil	30 ml	2 tbsp	2 tbsp
Large red onion, thinly sliced	1	1	1
Brown sugar	10 ml	2 tsp	2 tsp
Can of baked beans	420 g	15 oz	1 large
Beaujolais or other red wine	150 ml	¼ pt	⅔ cup
Beef stock	150 ml	¼ pt	⅔ cup
Salt and freshly ground black pepper			
Sprigs of fresh thyme	2	2	2
A sprig of fresh marjoram			
Buttered noodles, to serve			

① Cut the meat into strips about 2.5 cm × 10 cm/1 in × 4 in and toss in the seasoned flour.

② Heat the oil in a flameproof casserole dish (Dutch oven) and add the meat. Brown the meat on all sides, then lift out with a draining spoon and put to one side.

③ Add the onion to the pan and fry (sauté) until transparent.

④ Return the meat to the pan, then stir in the sugar, beans, wine and stock. Season to taste with salt and pepper, then add the herbs.

⑤ Cover and cook in a preheated oven at 180°C/350°F/gas mark 4 for about 1½ hours or until the meat is tender.

⑥ Serve with buttered noodles.

PREPARATION TIME: 10 MINUTES
COOKING TIME: 1¾ HOURS

GLAZED VENISON SAUSAGES IN BATTER

—— SERVES 4 ——

	METRIC	IMPERIAL	AMERICAN
Plain (all-purpose) flour	100 g	4 oz	1 cup
A pinch of salt			
Dried onion pieces	30 ml	2 tbsp	2 tbsp
Chopped fresh thyme	15 ml	1 tbsp	1 tbsp
Chopped fresh rosemary	15 ml	1 tbsp	1 tbsp
Egg	1	1	1
Wholegrain mustard	15 ml	1 tbsp	1 tbsp
Stout	300 ml	½ pt	1¼ cups
Oil	45 ml	3 tbsp	3 tbsp
Venison sausages	8	8	8
Redcurrant jelly (clear conserve)	40 ml	8 tsp	8 tsp
Creamed potatoes and broccoli, to serve			

① Make the batter by combining the flour, salt, dried onion and herbs. Make a well in the centre, then break in the egg, add the mustard and beat together, starting to incorporate some of the flour mixture.

② Gradually pour in the stout and beat well, incorporating the flour mixture to give a smooth batter. Leave to stand.

③ Heat the oil in a roasting tin (pan), then add the sausages and cook in a preheated oven at 230°C/450°F/gas mark 8 for about 10 minutes.

④ Remove from the oven, turn the sausages over and pour in the batter. Return to the oven and cook for about 30 minutes until risen and brown.

⑤ Spread the redcurrant jelly over each sausage and return to the oven for a few minutes.

⑥ Serve with creamed potatoes and broccoli.

PREPARATION TIME: 10 MINUTES
COOKING TIME: 45 MINUTES

SICILIAN VENISON CASSEROLE

—— SERVES 4 ——

	METRIC	IMPERIAL	AMERICAN
Extra virgin olive oil	30 ml	2 tbsp	2 tbsp
Boneless venison meat, diced	450 g	I lb	I lb
Red onions, quartered	4	4	4
Garlic cloves, halved	4	4	4
Button mushrooms, quartered	100 g	4 oz	4 oz
Plain (all-purpose) flour	15 ml	I tbsp	I tbsp
Red wine	300 ml	½ pt	1¼ cups
Sun-dried tomatoes	100 g	4 oz	4 oz
Stoned (pitted) black olives	75 g	3 oz	½ cup
A sprig of fresh thyme			
Dried rosemary	2.5 ml	½ tsp	½ tsp
Dried oregano	2.5 ml	½ tsp	½ tsp
Salt and freshly ground black pepper			
A sprig of fresh rosemary, to garnish			
Focaccia, to serve			

① Heat the oil in a flameproof casserole dish (Dutch oven) and brown the venison on all sides.

② Add the onions and garlic and fry (sauté) until lightly browned.

③ Stir in the mushrooms and cook until the juices start to run.

④ Blend in the flour, then gradually stir in the wine.

⑤ Add all the remaining ingredients and season to taste with salt and pepper.

⑥ Cover and place in a preheated oven at 140°C/275°F/gas mark 1 and cook for 2–2½ hours until the meat is tender.

⑦ Garnish with the rosemary sprig and serve with plenty of warm focaccia.

PREPARATION TIME: 15 MINUTES
COOKING TIME: 2¼ HOURS

POULTRY

Supermarkets nowadays sell a huge variety of ready-prepared poultry – skinned, boned and cut into convenient-sized portions. It's cheap too but, as you will see from the recipes here, it certainly doesn't have to be dull: try Chicken Blush (see page 72) or Chicken with Citrus Chilli Salsa (page 73), both simple but just that little bit different. Or for something special, Duck Breasts with Fig and Brandy Sauce (see page 83) makes a wonderful celebration dish.

CHICKEN AND PRAWN GUMBO
—— SERVES 4 ——

	METRIC	IMPERIAL	AMERICAN
Oil	60 ml	4 tbsp	4 tbsp
Boneless chicken, cut into bite-sized pieces	350 g	12 oz	12 oz
Spicy sausage, such as pepperoni, zywieska or salami, cut into bite-sized chunks	175 g	6 oz	6 oz
Smoked bacon, diced	100 g	4 oz	4 oz
Plain (all-purpose) flour	25 g	1 oz	¼ cup
Large onion, chopped	1	1	1
Celery stick, thinly sliced	1	1	1
Yellow (bell) pepper, seeded and chopped	1	1	1
Garlic cloves, crushed	2	2	2
Chicken stock	450 ml	¾ pt	2 cups
Creole seasoning	5 ml	1 tsp	1 tsp
Spring onions (scallions), sliced	4	4	4
Cooked, peeled prawns (shrimp), fresh or thawed frozen	225 g	8 oz	8 oz
Salt and freshly ground black pepper			
Shell-on prawns	8	8	8
Crusty bread, to serve			

① Heat about 30 ml/2 tbsp of the oil in a large frying pan (skillet), add the chicken and stir-fry until brown.

② Add the sausage and bacon and cook for a few more minutes. Remove with the chicken from the pan.

③ Add the remaining oil to the pan, then stir in the flour to make a paste.

④ Add the onion, celery, chopped pepper and garlic and stir constantly until all the vegetables are tender.

⑤ Return the meats to the pan and continue to stir for a few minutes. Gradually blend in the stock, bring to the boil, reduce the heat to a low simmer, stir in the seasoning and cook for about 45 minutes.

⑥ Stir in the spring onions, then the peeled prawns. Season to taste with salt and pepper and cook for a few more minutes to heat through.

⑦ Garnish with the whole prawns and serve accompanied by warm crusty bread.

PREPARATION TIME: 20 MINUTES
COOKING TIME: 1 HOUR AND 20 MINUTES

CHICKEN BLUSH

—— SERVES 4 ——

	METRIC	IMPERIAL	AMERICAN
Vegetable oil	15 ml	1 tbsp	1 tbsp
Large chicken breasts	4	4	4
Shallot, finely chopped	1	1	1
Chicken or vegetable stock	300 ml	½ pt	1¼ cups
Fresh or thawed frozen raspberries	75 g	3 oz	3 oz
Cornflour (cornstarch)	15 ml	1 tbsp	1 tbsp
Whipping cream	150 ml	¼ pt	⅔ cup
Green peppercorns, roughly crushed	15 ml	1 tbsp	1 tbsp
A pinch of salt			
Whole raspberries, for decoration	4	4	4
Creamed potatoes and petit pois, to serve			

① Heat the oil in a large, deep frying pan (skillet) or flameproof casserole dish (Dutch oven) and fry (sauté) the chicken breast on both sides until browned.

② Add the shallot and continue to cook for a few minutes.

③ Pour the stock over the chicken breasts. Cover and simmer for 20–30 minutes until the chicken is cooked through.

④ Meanwhile, liquidise the raspberries, then rub through a sieve (strainer) to remove the pips.

⑤ Blend the cornflour to a paste with a little water, then stir into the cooked chicken and continue to stir over a low heat until the sauce has thickened.

⑥ Stir in the raspberries, then reduce the heat and stir in the cream, being careful not to let the mixture boil.

⑦ Add the peppercorns and salt and heat through.

⑧ Serve the chicken breasts surrounded by a pool of raspberry cream sauce, garnished with a whole raspberry. Creamed potatoes and petit pois make ideal accompaniments.

PREPARATION TIME: 5 MINUTES
COOKING TIME: 50 MINUTES

CHICKEN WITH CITRUS CHILLI SALSA
—— SERVES 4 ——

	METRIC	IMPERIAL	AMERICAN
Extra virgin olive oil	15 ml	1 tbsp	1 tbsp
Chicken breast fillets	4	4	4
For the salsa:			
Green chilli, seeded and very finely chopped	1	1	1
Red chilli, seeded and very finely chopped	1	1	1
Red onion, very finely chopped	1	1	1
Finely chopped flesh of ½ orange			
Lime juice	15 ml	1 tbsp	1 tbsp
Soft brown sugar	10 ml	2 tsp	2 tsp
Salt and freshly ground black pepper			
Wild rice and French (green) beans, to serve			

① Heat the oil in a large frying pan (skillet) and fry (sauté) the chicken fillets for about 10–15 minutes, depending on their size, turning once.

② Meanwhile, combine all the salsa ingredients, seasoning to taste with salt and pepper.

③ Serve the chicken fillets with a spoonful of the salsa. Wild rice and French beans set off this dish very well.

PREPARATION TIME: 10 MINUTES
COOKING TIME: 15 MINUTES

THAI ROAST CHICKEN

—— SERVES 4 ——

	METRIC	IMPERIAL	AMERICAN
For the stuffing:			
Fresh breadcrumbs	100 g	4 oz	2 cups
Ginger purée (paste)	5 ml	1 tsp	1 tsp
Garlic purée	2.5 ml	½ tsp	½ tsp
Finely chopped fresh lemon grass	30 ml	2 tbsp	2 tbsp
Finely chopped fresh coriander (cilantro)	15 ml	1 tbsp	1 tbsp
Spring onions (scallions), finely chopped	4	4	4
Salt and freshly ground black pepper			
Butter, melted	50 g	2 oz	¼ cup
Chicken, fresh or thawed frozen	1.75 kg	4 lb	4 lb
For the rub:			
Ginger purée	15 ml	1 tbsp	1 tbsp
Garlic purée	5 ml	1 tsp	1 tsp
Five-spice powder	2.5 ml	½ tsp	½ tsp
Soy sauce	10 ml	2 tsp	2 tsp
Butter, softened	50 g	2 oz	¼ cup
Roast potatoes and stir-fried vegetables, to serve			

① Combine the breadcrumbs with all the other stuffing ingredients, binding well with the melted butter.

② Insert the stuffing into the neck of the chicken, pushing it up under the skin over the chicken breasts. Fold the neck skin over and secure with a skewer.

③ Weigh the chicken and place in a roasting tin (pan).

④ Combine all the ingredients for the rub except for the butter, adding salt sparingly as the soy sauce is quite salty. Rub all over the chicken skin. Spread the butter over the chicken, being generous with the breast area. Cover the pan loosely with kitchen foil.

⑤   Roast the chicken in a preheated oven at 200°C/400°F/ gas mark 6 for 20 minutes per 450 g/1 lb plus an extra 20 minutes, removing the foil for the final 20 minutes.

⑥   Allow the chicken to stand for a while before carving.

⑦   Serve with roast potatoes and stir-fried vegetables.

PREPARATION TIME: 30 MINUTES PLUS STANDING TIME
COOKING TIME: ABOUT 2 HOURS

CHICKEN WITH SMOKED HAM AND MUSHROOMS

—— SERVES 4 ——

	METRIC	IMPERIAL	AMERICAN
Oil	15 ml	1 tbsp	1 tbsp
Large chicken thighs	4	4	4
Large red onion, finely chopped	1	1	1
Chicken stock	300 ml	½ pt	1¼ cups
Salt and freshly ground black pepper			
Mushrooms, thinly sliced	75 g	3 oz	3 oz
Smoked ham, diced	75 g	3 oz	¾ cup
Vermouth	15 ml	1 tbsp	1 tbsp
Cornflour (cornstarch)	30 ml	2 tbsp	2 tbsp
Crème fraîche	150 ml	¼ pt	⅔ cup
Chopped fresh parsley	5 ml	1 tsp	1 tsp
New potatoes and broccoli, to serve			

① Heat the oil in a flameproof casserole dish (Dutch oven) and fry (sauté) the chicken thighs for about 10 minutes on each side or until well browned.

② Add the onion and fry briefly until softened.

③ Pour over the chicken stock and season with salt and pepper.

④ Cover the dish and cook in a preheated oven at 190°C/375°F/gas mark 5 for about 45 minutes or until the chicken is tender.

⑤ Remove the chicken from the casserole and keep warm.

⑥ Place the casserole on the hob, reheat the liquid and add the mushrooms. Stir in the smoked ham and vermouth.

⑦ Blend the cornflour with a little water, then stir the paste into the casserole and continue to stir over a moderate heat until thickened.

⑧ Stir in the crème fraîche, then return the chicken to the pan and heat through gently, without allowing the mixture to boil.

⑨ Garnish with the chopped parsley and serve with new potatoes and broccoli.

PREPARATION TIME: 5 MINUTES
COOKING TIME: 1 HOUR

SOUR CHICKEN WITH NOODLES
—— SERVES 4 ——

	METRIC	IMPERIAL	AMERICAN
Boneless chicken meat, diced	350 g	12 oz	12 oz
Greek yoghurt	30 ml	2 tbsp	2 tbsp
Indian lime pickle	30 ml	2 tbsp	2 tbsp
Oil	15 ml	1 tbsp	1 tbsp
Garlic cloves, crushed	2	2	2
Large onion, sliced	1	1	1
Button mushrooms, quartered	100 g	4 oz	4 oz
Water	300 ml	½ pt	1¼ cups
Cabbage, finely shredded	225 g	8 oz	8 oz
Medium egg noodles	125 g	4½ oz	4½ oz
Sweet fruity salad, to serve			

① Combine the chicken with the yoghurt and pickle and leave to marinate for at least 30 minutes.

② Heat the oil in a deep, lidded frying pan (skillet) or lidded wok. Add the garlic and onion and fry until soft.

③ Add the meat and stir-fry for about 10 minutes. Reserve the marinade mixture.

④ Stir in the mushrooms and cook until soft.

⑤ Combine the water with the remaining marinade mixture and pour into the pan. Bring to the boil, then stir in the cabbage and noodles. Reduce the heat, cover and simmer for about 15 minutes.

⑥ Serve with a sweet fruity salad to balance the sourness of this dish.

PREPARATION TIME: 15 MINUTES PLUS MARINATING
COOKING TIME: 35 MINUTES

CHICKEN WITH PICKLED WALNUTS AND MUSHROOMS

—— SERVES 4 ——

	METRIC	IMPERIAL	AMERICAN
Plain (all-purpose) flour	45 ml	3 tbsp	3 tbsp
Salt and freshly ground black pepper			
Chicken portions	4	4	4
Oil	15 ml	I tbsp	I tbsp
Small onions, quartered	4	4	4
Button mushrooms, quartered	175 g	6 oz	6 oz
Pickled walnut vinegar	90 ml	6 tbsp	6 tbsp
Pickled walnuts, sliced	6	6	6
Water	60 ml	4 tbsp	4 tbsp
Soft brown sugar	5 ml	I tsp	I tsp
Creamed potatoes and baby carrots, to serve			

① Season the flour with salt and pepper, then toss the chicken in the flour.

② Heat the oil in a flameproof casserole dish (Dutch oven) and fry (sauté) the onions until slightly softened. Remove from the pan with a draining spoon.

③ Add the chicken to the pan and fry until browned on all sides.

④ Return the onions to the pan, add the mushrooms and cook for a few minutes.

⑤ Stir in all the remaining ingredients, then cover tightly with a lid or foil and cook in a preheated oven at 190°C/375°F/gas mark 5 for about 45 minutes.

⑥ Remove the cover and return to the oven for 10–15 minutes until the upper chicken skin is crisp.

⑦ Serve with creamed potatoes and baby carrots.

PREPARATION TIME: 10 MINUTES
COOKING TIME: 1 HOUR AND 10 MINUTES

WARM SALAD OF CHICKEN LIVERS WITH WATERCRESS

—— SERVES 4 ——

	METRIC	IMPERIAL	AMERICAN
No-need-to-soak dried prunes, finely chopped	75 g	3 oz	½ cup
Sherry vinegar	60 ml	4 tbsp	4 tbsp
Oil	15 ml	1 tbsp	1 tbsp
Chicken livers, trimmed and roughly chopped	225 g	8 oz	8 oz
Spring onions (scallions), cut into short lengths	6	6	6
Bunches of watercress, trimmed	2	2	2
Extra virgin olive oil	45 ml	3 tbsp	3 tbsp
Salt and freshly ground black pepper			
Warm ciabatta, to serve			

① Place the chopped prunes in a bowl and pour on the vinegar. Allow to soak for at least 30 minutes.

② Heat the oil in a frying pan (skillet) and add the chicken livers. Fry (sauté) over a low heat, turning frequently, until they are browned and the juices run clear.

③ Add the spring onions, stir-fry quickly, then remove the pan from the heat.

④ Place the watercress in a serving dish, then add the chicken liver mixture, drizzle with the prune vinegar and olive oil and season to taste. Toss together and serve at once with warm ciabatta.

PREPARATION TIME: 5 MINUTES PLUS 30 MINUTES SOAKING TIME
COOKING TIME: 10 MINUTES

SMOKED CHICKEN SALAD WITH AVOCADO

—— SERVES 4 ——

	METRIC	IMPERIAL	AMERICAN
Smoked cooked chicken or turkey, cut into bite-sized chunks	350 g	12 oz	3 cups
Strawberries, hulled and thickly sliced	100 g	4 oz	4 oz
Large avocado, stoned (pitted), skinned and diced	1	1	1
Small red onion, very finely chopped	½	½	½
Sunflower seeds, toasted	25 g	1 oz	¼ cup
Balsamic vinegar	30 ml	2 tbsp	2 tbsp
Raspberry or strawberry vinegar	15 ml	1 tbsp	1 tbsp
Walnut oil	30 ml	2 tbsp	2 tbsp
Green peppercorns, crushed	5 ml	1 tsp	1 tsp
Salt			
Crusty breads, to serve			

① Carefully combine the chicken or turkey, strawberries, avocado, onion and sunflower seeds.

② Mix together the remaining ingredients, adding salt to taste, then gently stir into the chicken mixture.

③ Pile on to plates and serve. This exotic salad needs little more than a selection of crusty breads to go with it.

PREPARATION TIME: 10 MINUTES
COOKING TIME: NONE

TURKEY AND CHESTNUT FEAST
—— SERVES 4 ——

	METRIC	IMPERIAL	AMERICAN
Oil	15 ml	1 tbsp	1 tbsp
Large onion, thinly sliced	1	1	1
Cocktail sausages	225 g	8 oz	8 oz
Cold cooked turkey meat, cut into bite-sized pieces	350 g	12 oz	3 cups
Chestnuts, peeled and halved	8	8	8
Cold turkey gravy	600 ml	1 pt	2½ cups
Cranberry sauce or jelly (clear conserve)	45 ml	3 tbsp	3 tbsp
Salt and freshly ground black pepper			
Creamed potatoes and baby carrots, to serve			

① Heat the oil in a large frying pan (skillet) and gently fry (sauté) the onion until soft.

② Add the sausages and cook, turning until browned on all sides.

③ Stir in the turkey, chestnuts and gravy and heat through until bubbling.

④ Reduce the heat slightly and stir in the cranberry sauce or jelly. Season to taste, then cover and simmer for about 10 minutes.

⑤ Serve with creamed potatoes and baby carrots.

PREPARATION TIME: 5 MINUTES
COOKING TIME: 30 MINUTES

SUNNY TURKEY ESCALOPES
—— SERVES 4 ——

	METRIC	IMPERIAL	AMERICAN
Olive oil	15 ml	I tbsp	I tbsp
Clear honey	15 ml	I tbsp	I tbsp
Dijon mustard	15 ml	I tbsp	I tbsp
Salt and freshly ground black pepper			
Turkey escalopes, lightly beaten	4	4	4
Crème fraîche	60 ml	4 tbsp	4 tbsp
Snipped fresh chives	15 ml	I tbsp	I tbsp
Buttered noodles and green salad, to serve			

① Combine the oil, honey, mustard and seasoning and brush on one side of each of the escalopes.

② Heat a large frying pan (skillet) and place the meat, dressed-side down, in the pan. Cook gently for about 5 minutes.

③ Brush the other side of the turkey pieces with the dressing, turn them over and cook for a further 5 minutes or until the meat juices run clear.

④ Pour any remaining dressing into the pan and warm through, then add the crème fraîche and warm through, stirring constantly. Do not allow the mixture to boil.

⑤ Serve the turkey with a pool of the sauce and a scattering of chives, accompanied by buttered noodles and a crisp green salad.

PREPARATION TIME: 5 MINUTES
COOKING TIME: 15 MINUTES

DUCK BREASTS WITH FIG AND BRANDY SAUCE

—— SERVES 4 ——

	METRIC	IMPERIAL	AMERICAN
No-need-to-soak dried figs, roughly chopped	100 g	4 oz	⅔ cup
Brandy	90 ml	6 tbsp	6 tbsp
Duck breasts	4	4	4
Olive oil	15 ml	1 tbsp	1 tbsp
Salt and freshly ground black pepper			
Buttery Potato, Swede and Apple Bake (see page 102), to serve			

① Put the figs in a bowl and pour on the brandy. Leave to soak for at least 30 minutes.

② Using a very sharp knife, make several diagonal cuts in the skin of each duck breast.

③ Heat the olive oil in a flameproof dish and brown the duck breasts for a few minutes on each side. Place the dish in a preheated oven and cook at 230°C/450°F/gas mark 8 for 10–15 minutes until the duck is crisp and the juices run clear. Remove from the pan and keep warm.

④ Pour off any fat and place the dish on the heat. Pour in the figs and brandy and bring to the boil. Reduce the heat and simmer gently for a few minutes. Season to taste.

⑤ Pour the sauce over the duck and serve with a helping of Buttery Potato, Swede and Apple Bake.

PREPARATION TIME: 5 MINUTES PLUS ½ HOUR SOAKING TIME
COOKING TIME: 25 MINUTES

DUCK AND APRICOT PILAU
—— SERVES 4 ——

	METRIC	IMPERIAL	AMERICAN
Olive oil	45 ml	3 tbsp	3 tbsp
Large red onion, finely chopped	1	1	1
Garlic cloves, crushed	2	2	2
Red chilli, seeded and finely chopped	1	1	1
Boneless duck meat, cut into thin strips	350 g	12 oz	12 oz
Bulghar (cracked) wheat	225 g	8 oz	2 cups
Vegetable stock or water	300 ml	½ pt	1¼ cups
Canned apricot halves, roughly chopped	8	8	8
Flaked (slivered) almonds	50 g	2 oz	½ cup
Salt and freshly ground black pepper			
Finely chopped fresh coriander (cilantro)	10 ml	2 tsp	2 tsp

① Heat the oil in a deep frying pan (skillet) or saucepan and add the onion, garlic and chilli. Fry (sauté) until tender, then remove from the pan.

② Add the duck to the pan and stir-fry until browned.

③ Stir in the bulghar wheat, then stir over a low heat for about 30 seconds until the grains are coated in oil.

④ Add the stock or water. Bring to the boil, cover and simmer for 5–10 minutes until the wheat grains are softened and the liquid has been absorbed.

⑤ Return the onion mixture to the pan with the apricots and nuts. Season to taste with salt and pepper, then heat through.

⑥ Serve hot, sprinkled with fresh chopped coriander.

PREPARATION TIME: 10 MINUTES
COOKING TIME: 20 MINUTES

DUCK WITH CARAMELISED APPLES
—— SERVES 2 ——

	METRIC	IMPERIAL	AMERICAN
Oil	5 ml	I tsp	I tsp
Butter	50 g	2 oz	¼ cup
Medium duck breasts	2	2	2
Apple juice	120 ml	4 fl oz	½ cup
Salt and freshly ground black pepper			
Eating (dessert) apples, cored and thickly sliced	2	2	2
Granulated sugar	60 ml	4 tbsp	4 tbsp
New potatoes and creamed parsnips, to serve			

① Heat the oil and half the butter in a frying pan (skillet) and fry (sauté) the duck breasts for about 5 minutes, turning once.

② Pour over the apple juice, season with salt and pepper and simmer gently for about 10 minutes.

③ Transfer the duck and sauce to a serving dish and keep warm.

④ Melt the remaining butter and use to brush the apple slices, then dip them in the sugar and place them in the hot pan.

⑤ Cook until the sugar melts and browns, then turn the slices to caramelise the other side.

⑥ Pour the apple sauce around the duck and top with the caramelised apples.

⑦ Serve with new potatoes and creamed parsnips.

PREPARATION TIME: 5 MINUTES
COOKING TIME: 25 MINUTES

DUCK LEGS IN PLUM AND NUT TROUSERS

—— SERVES 4 ——

	METRIC	IMPERIAL	AMERICAN
Duck legs	4	4	4
Salt			
Can of plums in syrup	410 g	14½ oz	1 large
Ground almonds	90 g	6 tbsp	6 tbsp
Clear honey	10 ml	2 tsp	2 tsp
Cashew nuts, coarsely chopped	60 ml	4 tbsp	4 tbsp
Freshly ground black pepper			
Chilli powder	2.5 ml	½ tsp	½ tsp
Sherry	45 ml	3 tbsp	3 tbsp
Arrowroot	10 ml	2 tsp	2 tsp
New potatoes and spring greens (collard greens), to serve			

① With the flat side down, loosen the skin on the duck legs upwards from the wide end of the leg to create a pocket. Prick the duck skin well and rub all over with salt.

② Drain the plums and reserve the syrup. Chop the plums finely.

③ Mix the almonds, honey, cashew nuts, salt and pepper and chilli powder into the chopped plums, then divide the mixture between the four duck legs, spooning carefully into the pockets. Close the pockets and secure with fine skewers to hold in the stuffing. Place in a roasting tin (pan) and cook in a preheated oven at 190°C/375°F/gas mark 5 for about 50 minutes.

④ Meanwhile, combine the reserved syrup with the sherry and arrowroot.

⑤ Transfer the duck to a serving dish and keep warm. Place the roasting tin on the hob and pour in the syrup mixture. Heat to simmering point, stirring constantly, until the sauce is thickened.

⑥ Pour a pool of sauce around the duck legs and serve with new potatoes and spring greens.

PREPARATION TIME: 15 MINUTES
COOKING TIME: 55 MINUTES

VEGETABLE DISHES

This section contains a selection of my favourite vegetable dishes, both main courses and accompaniments. Please note, though, that many of the side dishes will make delicious light lunch or supper dishes, served with a crisp salad or perhaps some crusty bread.

NESTS OF VEGETABLES IN BALSAMIC VINEGAR

—— SERVES 4 ——

	METRIC	IMPERIAL	AMERICAN
Whole baby sweetcorn (corn) cobs	8	8	8
Shallots, halved	8	8	8
Baby carrots, washed	12	12	12
Mangetout (snow peas), topped and tailed	50 g	2 oz	2 oz
French (green) beans, topped and tailed	100 g	4 oz	4 oz
Extra virgin olive oil	20 ml	4 tsp	4 tsp
Balsamic vinegar	45 ml	3 tbsp	3 tbsp
Roughly chopped fresh marjoram	60 ml	4 tbsp	4 tbsp
Roughly chopped fresh mint	60 ml	4 tbsp	4 tbsp
Salt and freshly ground black pepper			

① Cut eight circles of greaseproof (waxed) paper measuring about 25 cm/10 in across. Place the circles together in pairs so that there are four circles of double thickness.

② Divide all the vegetables between the four circles, placing them on one half of each circle. Drizzle the olive oil and vinegar over, then sprinkle with the herbs. Season to taste with salt and pepper.

③ Fold each circle in half and seal in the food by tightly rolling and folding the edges to make well-sealed parcels. Place the 'nests' in a steamer and cover with a tight-fitting lid.

④ Steam over boiling water for about 10 minutes.

⑤ Serve the nests on individual plates just slightly opened so that the juices and aroma can seep out.

PREPARATION TIME: 20 MINUTES
COOKING TIME: 10 MINUTES

GREEN POTATOES

This dish makes an excellent accompaniment to grilled (broiled) gammon.

—— SERVES 4 ——

	METRIC	IMPERIAL	AMERICAN
Butter	45 ml	3 tbsp	3 tbsp
Large leek, finely chopped	I	I	I
Spinach, roughly shredded	100 g	4 oz	4 oz
Large potatoes, peeled and cut into chunks	4	4	4
Milk	45 ml	3 tbsp	3 tbsp
Salt and freshly ground black pepper			
Grated nutmeg	2.5 ml	½ tsp	½ tsp

① Heat 15 ml/1 tbsp of the butter in a saucepan and add the leek and spinach. Cover and fry (sauté) very gently for about 5 minutes until soft, stirring occasionally. Transfer to a plate and keep warm.

② Place the potatoes in the pan and cover with water. Bring to the boil, cover the pan and simmer until the potatoes are very soft.

③ Drain off the water, then add the remaining butter and milk and mash well. Stir in the leek and spinach and warm through. Season with salt, pepper and nutmeg and serve.

PREPARATION TIME: 10 MINUTES
COOKING TIME: 30 MINUTES

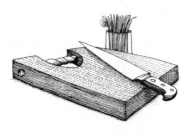

BAKED SQUASH WITH SUN-DRIED TOMATOES

Try this with cold cooked meats and fresh crusty bread.

—— SERVES 4 ——

	METRIC	IMPERIAL	AMERICAN
Large squash	1	1	1
Salt			
Extra virgin olive oil	15 ml	1 tbsp	1 tbsp
Sun-dried tomatoes, roughly chopped	100 g	4 oz	4 oz
Green peppercorns, roughly crushed	15 ml	1 tbsp	1 tbsp

① Wrap the squash in kitchen foil and place in a roasting tin (pan) in a preheated oven at 190°C/375°F/gas mark 5 for 45–60 minutes or until the flesh feels soft when a skewer is inserted.

② Remove the foil and halve the squash lengthways. Scoop out the seeds and discard.

③ Cut each half lengthways to give four pieces. Sprinkle with the salt and drizzle over the olive oil. Spread the tomatoes over each piece of squash and sprinkle with the crushed peppercorns. Return the squash to the oven for 10–15 minutes to heat through before serving.

PREPARATION TIME: 5 MINUTES
COOKING TIME: 1–1¼ HOURS

QUICK GARLIC AND MUSHROOM SPINACH

This is a lovely accompaniment to lamb chops.

—— SERVES 4 ——

	METRIC	IMPERIAL	AMERICAN
Butter	15 ml	1 tbsp	1 tbsp
Extra virgin olive oil	15 ml	1 tbsp	1 tbsp
Garlic cloves, crushed	2	2	2
Shallots, thinly sliced	3	3	3
Dried thyme	2.5 ml	½ tsp	½ tsp
Button mushrooms, quartered	100 g	4 oz	4 oz
Fresh baby leaf spinach	450 g	1 lb	1 lb
Salt and freshly ground black pepper			

① Heat the butter and olive oil in a large saucepan. Add the garlic and shallots and cook for several minutes until softened.

② Stir in the thyme and mushrooms and cook until the mushrooms are tender and the juices starting to run.

③ Add the spinach and stir until it has sunk down and wilted. Season generously with salt and pepper and serve at once.

PREPARATION TIME: 5 MINUTES
COOKING TIME: 10 MINUTES

ROAST VEGETABLES WITH SUN-DRIED TOMATOES
—— SERVES 4 ——

	METRIC	IMPERIAL	AMERICAN
Aubergine (eggplant), thickly sliced	1	1	1
Salt			
Small shallots	16	16	16
Garlic cloves	8	8	8
Medium courgettes (zucchini), cut into long thick slices	2	2	2
Small red (bell) pepper, seeded and quartered	1	1	1
Small green pepper, seeded and quartered	1	1	1
Large fennel bulb, trimmed and cut into 8 pieces	1	1	1
Sprigs of fresh rosemary	4	4	4
Sprigs of fresh thyme	4	4	4
Extra virgin olive oil	60 ml	4 tbsp	4 tbsp
Salt and freshly ground black pepper			
Black olives, stoned (pitted)	12	12	12
Sun-dried tomatoes	16	16	16
Soft polenta (cornmeal) and green salad, to serve			

① Place the aubergine in a bowl, sprinkle with salt and leave to stand for 20 minutes.

② Drain the aubergine and rinse well in cold running water. Pat dry on kitchen paper (paper towels).

③ Place all the vegetables except the olives and tomatoes in a roasting tin (pan) and add the herbs and olive oil. Season well with salt and pepper, then toss the vegetables in the oil and seasoning. Cook in a preheated oven at 200°C/400°F/gas mark 6 for 15 minutes.

④ Add the olives and tomatoes, stir well and return to the oven for 10 minutes.

⑤ Serve with polenta and a crisp green salad.

PREPARATION TIME: 10 MINUTES
COOKING TIME: 25 MINUTES

PUMPKIN TAGINE

—— SERVES 4 ——

	METRIC	IMPERIAL	AMERICAN
Oil	30 ml	2 tbsp	2 tbsp
Large onion, finely chopped	1	1	1
Garlic clove, crushed	1	1	1
Pumpkin, peeled, seeded and cut into bite-sized cubes	450 g	1 lb	1 lb
Red (bell) pepper, seeded and diced	1	1	1
Can of chopped tomatoes	410 g	14½ oz	1 large
Sun-dried tomato purée (paste)	15 ml	1 tbsp	1 tbsp
Ground cinnamon	5 ml	1 tsp	1 tsp
Bay leaf	1	1	1
Vegetable stock	150 ml	¼ pt	⅔ cup
Can of green lentils, drained	400 g	14 oz	1 large
Sultanas (golden raisins)	50 g	2 oz	⅓ cup
Blanched almonds, roughly chopped	50 g	2 oz	½ cup
Salt and freshly ground black pepper			
Crusty bread, to serve			

① Heat the oil in a large lidded saucepan and stir-fry the onion and garlic until very soft.

② Add the pumpkin and red pepper and fry (sauté) gently for about 5 minutes.

③ Stir in the remaining ingredients, seasoning to taste with salt and pepper. Cover the pan, reduce to a simmer and cook for about 30 minutes until the pumpkin is very tender.

④ Serve warm with fresh crusty bread.

PREPARATION TIME: 15 MINUTES
COOKING TIME: 40 MINUTES

CELERY HEARTS WITH MELTING GOATS' CHEESE

—— SERVES 4 ——

	METRIC	IMPERIAL	AMERICAN
Cans of celery hearts, drained	2 × 400 g	2 × 14 oz	2 large
Vegetable stock (bouillon) cube	I	I	I
Boiling water	150 ml	¼ pt	⅔ cup
White wine	30 ml	2 tbsp	2 tbsp
Small sprigs of fresh rosemary	4	4	4
Salt and freshly ground black pepper			
Goats' cheese log, cut into four thick slices	350 g	12 oz	12 oz
French bread, to serve			

① Spread the celery hearts over the base of an ovenproof dish.

② Dissolve the stock cube in the boiling water, add the wine, then pour over the celery.

③ Scatter the rosemary over and season generously.

④ Place the four goats' cheese slices on the surface of the celery.

⑤ Cook in a preheated oven at 180°C/350°F/gas mark 4 for 15–20 minutes until piping hot and the goats' cheese is beginning to melt over the celery.

⑥ Serve hot with French bread.

PREPARATION TIME: 3 MINUTES
COOKING TIME: 20 MINUTES

CREAMY SWEETCORN IN A WALNUT CRUST
—— SERVES 4 ——

	METRIC	IMPERIAL	AMERICAN
Plain (all-purpose) flour	175 g	6 oz	1½ cups
A pinch of salt			
Margarine or butter	75 g	3 oz	⅓ cup
Walnut pieces, finely chopped	45 ml	3 tbsp	3 tbsp
Small leek, very finely shredded	1	1	1
Walnut halves	25 g	1 oz	¼ cup
Salt and freshly ground black pepper			
Can of creamed sweetcorn (corn)	418 g	14½ oz	1 large
Fourme d'Ambert cheese, very thinly sliced	75 g	3 oz	3 oz
A little milk, for brushing			
A selection of salads, to serve			

① Sift the flour with the salt into a large bowl, then rub in the butter or margarine until the mixture has the consistency of fine breadcrumbs. Stir in the walnut pieces, then stir in enough water to bring the mixture together and give a soft but not sticky dough.

② On a lightly floured board, roll out about half the dough and use to line a 20 cm/8 in shallow pie dish or sandwich tin (pan).

③ Place the leek in the bottom of the pie, then arrange the walnut halves over the top. Season well with salt and pepper. Pour over the sweetcorn and season again. Top with the slices of cheese.

④ Roll out the remaining pastry (paste) and place on the top of the pie, sealing the 'lid' by damping the edges. Brush the surface carefully with a little milk. Bake in a preheated oven at 200°C/400°F/gas mark 6 for about 20 minutes until golden brown.

⑤ Serve hot or cold with a selection of salads.

PREPARATION TIME: 20 MINUTES
COOKING TIME: 20 MINUTES

AUBERGINE AND RED ONION OMELETTE

—— SERVES 1 ——

	METRIC	IMPERIAL	AMERICAN
Small aubergine (eggplant), thinly sliced	½	½	½
Salt			
Oil	45 ml	3 tbsp	3 tbsp
Garlic clove, crushed	1	1	1
Small red onion, thinly sliced	1	1	1
Cold cooked peas	30 ml	2 tbsp	2 tbsp
Small cold cooked potato, diced	1	1	1
Medium curry paste	15 ml	1 tbsp	1 tbsp
Eggs, lightly beaten	3	3	3
Freshly ground black pepper			
Chopped fresh coriander (cilantro)	10 ml	2 tsp	2 tsp
Cucumber raita and naan bread, to serve			

① Lay the aubergine on a plate, sprinkle with salt and leave to stand for about 20 minutes.

② Rinse well in cold running water, then pat dry on kitchen paper (paper towels).

③ Heat the oil in a medium frying pan (skillet) and fry (sauté) the aubergine on both sides until lightly browned.

④ Add the garlic and onion and stir-fry until soft.

⑤ Stir in the peas, potato and curry paste and heat through.

⑥ Season the eggs to taste with salt and pepper, then pour into the pan to cover the cooked vegetables, swirling the pan to ensure the egg is evenly distributed.

⑦ When the egg is nearly set on the surface, sprinkle over the coriander. Fold the omelette in half with a fish slice and serve immediately with a cucumber raita and warm naan bread.

PREPARATION TIME: 10 MINUTES
COOKING TIME: 15 MINUTES

BAKED STUFFED ONIONS WITH LENTILS

This makes a perfect accompaniment to lamb chops, with creamed potatoes.

—— SERVES 4 ——

	METRIC	IMPERIAL	AMERICAN
Large Spanish onions	4	4	4
Vegetable stock (bouillon) cube	I	I	I
Canned green lentils, drained	45 ml	3 tbsp	3 tbsp
Mushrooms, very finely chopped	4	4	4
Garlic cloves, crushed	2	2	2
Very finely chopped canned jalapeño chillis	10 ml	2 tsp	2 tsp
Clear honey	15 ml	I tbsp	I tbsp
Tomato purée (paste)	10 ml	2 tsp	2 tsp
Salt and freshly ground black pepper			

① Trim the ends off the peeled onions and stand them in an ovenproof dish. Crumble the stock cube around them. Pour in enough boiling water to come about one-third of the way up the onions. Cover, place in a preheated oven and cook at 190°C/375°F/gas mark 5 for about 30 minutes.

② Meanwhile, combine all the remaining ingredients, seasoning to taste with salt and pepper.

③ Remove the onions from the oven and gently squeeze out the centres. Finely chop the onion centres and mix into the stuffing mixture. Spoon the mixture back into the onion shells and return them to the dish.

④ Cover the dish and return to the oven for about 1½ hours or until the onion flesh is very tender.

PREPARATION TIME: 20 MINUTES
COOKING TIME: 2 HOURS

BALTI MIXED VEGETABLE CURRY

—— SERVES 4 ——

	METRIC	IMPERIAL	AMERICAN
Oil	10 ml	2 tsp	2 tsp
Cumin seeds	2.5 ml	½ tsp	½ tsp
Ground turmeric	1.5 ml	¼ tsp	¼ tsp
Garlic cloves, finely chopped	4	4	4
Onion, finely chopped	100 g	4 oz	4 oz
Aubergine (eggplant), diced	175 g	6 oz	6 oz
Balti masala paste	30 ml	2 tbsp	2 tbsp
Frozen sweetcorn (corn)	175 g	6 oz	6 oz
Can of chick peas (garbanzos), drained	150 g	5 oz	1 small
Can of lentils, drained	150 g	5 oz	1 small
Brinjal (aubergine) pickle	30 ml	2 tbsp	2 tbsp
Baby leaf spinach	175 g	6 oz	6 oz
Cherry tomatoes, halved	6	6	6
Fresh red chillis, seeded and finely chopped	2	2	2
Garam masala	7.5 ml	1½ tsp	1½ tsp
Fresh chopped coriander (cilantro)	30 ml	2 tbsp	2 tbsp
Salt			
Pilau rice, to serve			

① Heat the oil in a wok or large heavy-based frying pan (skillet) and stir-fry the cumin seeds and turmeric for about 30 seconds.

② Add the garlic and onion and fry until the onion is browned.

③ Add the aubergine and fry until soft.

④ Stir in the balti masala paste and cook for several minutes.

⑤ Add all the remaining ingredients, seasoning to taste with salt. Stir well and heat through.

⑥ Serve with pilau rice.

PREPARATION TIME: 15 MINUTES
COOKING TIME: 10 MINUTES

CARAMELISED ONION AND ARTICHOKE FLAN

—— SERVES 4 ——

	METRIC	IMPERIAL	AMERICAN
Frozen puff pastry (paste), thawed	350 g	12 oz	12 oz
Caramelised onions, from a jar	90 ml	6 tbsp	6 tbsp
Can of artichoke hearts, drained and roughly chopped	400 g	14 oz	1 large
Black olives, pitted (stoned)	16	16	16
Chopped thyme	15 ml	1 tbsp	1 tbsp
Green peppercorns, roughly crushed	15 ml	1 tbsp	1 tbsp
Coarse salt			
Olive oil	15 ml	1 tbsp	1 tbsp
Tomato and mixed leaf salad, to serve			

① Roll out the pastry on a floured surface to a 25 cm/10 in square and place on a baking (cookie) sheet. Score a border round the pastry about 2.5 cm/1 in from the edge, then prick all over the central area with a fork.

② Spread the caramelised onions over the pricked area, then top with the chopped artichoke and scatter the olives over. Sprinkle with the chopped thyme, crushed peppercorns and salt. Drizzle the olive oil over the surface.

③ Bake in a preheated oven at 200°C/400°F/gas mark 6 for about 20–25 minutes until puffy and browned.

④ Serve hot or cold with a tomato and mixed leaf salad.

PREPARATION TIME: 10 MINUTES
COOKING TIME: 25 MINUTES

LEEK AND LENTIL RISOTTO WITH CHEESE
—— SERVES 4 ——

	METRIC	IMPERIAL	AMERICAN
Olive oil	30 ml	2 tbsp	2 tbsp
Rashers (slices) of smoked streaky bacon, finely chopped	6	6	6
Medium leeks, trimmed and very finely chopped	2	2	2
Garlic cloves, crushed	2	2	2
Arborio rice	225 g	8 oz	I cup
Boiling water	750 ml	I¼ pts	3 cups
Vegetable stock (bouillon) cube	I	I	I
Dried thyme	5 ml	I tsp	I tsp
Split red lentils	75 g	3 oz	½ cup
Salt and freshly ground black pepper			
Strong Cheddar cheese, grated	100 g	4 oz	I cup
Roughly chopped fresh thyme	5 ml	I tsp	I tsp
Tomato, apple and cucumber salad, to serve			

① Heat the oil in a deep frying pan (skillet) or large saucepan and add the bacon, leeks and garlic. Stir-fry for about 5 minutes until softened.

② Stir in the rice and cook for a few minutes so that the grains are glossy.

③ Pour in the water and stir well. Crumble in the stock cube and add the thyme, lentils and salt and pepper. Simmer for about 15 minutes until the rice is tender and the liquid has been absorbed.

④ Quickly stir in the grated cheese and serve garnished with the chopped thyme.

⑤ Serve with a tomato, apple and cucumber salad.

PREPARATION TIME: 15 MINUTES
COOKING TIME: 30 MINUTES

CRUSTY BREAD WITH A WILD MUSHROOM FILLING

—— SERVES 4 ——

	METRIC	IMPERIAL	AMERICAN
Medium loaf of crusty bread	1	1	1
Butter, softened	50 g	2 oz	¼ cup
Garlic cloves, crushed	2	2	2
Wholegrain mustard	15 ml	1 tbsp	1 tbsp
Salt and freshly ground black pepper			
Jar of antipasto wild mushrooms, drained and roughly chopped, reserving the oil	290 g	10½ oz	1 medium
Mozzarella cheese, cut into thin slices	225 g	8 oz	8 oz
Selection of salads, to serve			

① Slice almost through the loaf, making slices of medium thickness and leaving them just connected at the bottom.

② Combine the butter with the garlic, mustard and salt and pepper to taste and spread over one side of each slice of bread. Roughly spread the mushrooms over the top of the butter. Pack the slices of cheese between the slices of bread.

③ Place the whole loaf on a large sheet of silver foil; brush the bread with a little of the reserved oil, then wrap well, rolling the foil at the edges to secure.

④ Place in a preheated oven and cook at 200°C/400°F/gas mark 6 for about 30 minutes until the cheese has melted and the bread is crispy.

⑤ Serve with a selection of salads.

PREPARATION TIME: 20 MINUTES
COOKING TIME: 30 MINUTES

BUTTERY POTATO, SWEDE AND APPLE BAKE

This dish makes an ideal accompaniment to Duck Breasts with Figs and Brandy (see page 83).

—— SERVES 4 ——

	METRIC	IMPERIAL	AMERICAN
Butter	100 g	4 oz	½ cup
Potatoes, peeled and very thinly sliced	700 g	1½ lb	1½ lb
Swede (rutabaga), very thinly sliced	350 g	12 oz	12 oz
Large eating (dessert) apple, peeled and sliced	1	1	1
Golden (light corn) syrup	30 ml	2 tbsp	2 tbsp
Worcestershire sauce	10 ml	2 tsp	2 tsp
Salt and freshly ground black pepper			

① Brush the inside of a 20 cm/8 in round deep dish or tin (pan) liberally with butter. Melt the remaining butter.

② Divide the potato into four piles and the swede into two.

③ Cover the bottom of the dish with a layer of potato, then brush with butter. Place a layer of swede on top.

④ Combine the syrup with the Worcestershire sauce and use half to brush over the swede. Cover with another layer of potato and brush with butter. Use all the apple for the next layer and brush with butter.

⑤ Repeat the layering, brushing the swede layer with butter and the syrup mixture.

⑥ Pour the remaining butter all over the top, then season well with salt and pepper. Cover well with kitchen foil, then place in a preheated oven and cook at 200°C/400°F/ gas mark 6 for 40 minutes.

⑦ Remove the foil and cook for a further 5–10 minutes to brown the surface.

⑧ Serve hot with the buttery juices.

PREPARATION TIME: 20 MINUTES
COOKING TIME: 50 MINUTES

PESTO LINGUINE WITH WALNUTS, OLIVES AND FETA
—— SERVES 4 ——

	METRIC	IMPERIAL	AMERICAN
Dried linguine	400 g	14 oz	14 oz
Ready-made pesto	90 ml	6 tbsp	6 tbsp
Walnut pieces	100 g	4 oz	1 cup
Black olives, stoned (pitted)	6	6	6
Green olives, stoned	6	6	6
Feta cheese, roughly diced	175 g	6 oz	1½ cups
Salt and freshly ground black pepper			
Torn fresh basil leaves	30 ml	2 tbsp	2 tbsp
Italian bread, to serve			

① Bring a large saucepan of salted water to the boil and cook the linguine for 8–10 minutes until just tender. Drain well and return to the pan.

② Stir in the pesto, walnuts, olives and half the cheese and season to taste with salt and pepper. Heat through, stirring.

③ Top with the remaining cheese and the basil leaves and serve with plenty of warm Italian bread.

PREPARATION TIME: 10 MINUTES
COOKING TIME: 15 MINUTES

JACKET POTATOES WITH RED PESTO

—— SERVES 4 ——

	METRIC	IMPERIAL	AMERICAN
Large potatoes, scrubbed and pricked all over	4	4	4
Butter	25 g	1 oz	2 tbsp
Ready-made red pesto	90 ml	6 tbsp	6 tbsp
Large beefsteak tomato, sliced	1	1	1
Beansprouts, washed	50 g	2 oz	2 oz
Extra virgin olive oil	15 ml	1 tbsp	1 tbsp
Coarse salt			
Freshly ground black pepper			
Mozzarella cheese, thinly sliced	100 g	4 oz	4 oz
Selection of salads, to serve			

① Bake the potatoes in a preheated oven at 200°C/400°F/ gas mark 6 for about 1½ hours until they are soft inside and crisp on the outside.

② Make a vertical cut down through the potatoes but leave the bottom part of the skin joined. Scoop out the hot potato flesh and mash with the butter and red pesto.

③ Pile the mixture back into the potato halves, then place slices of tomato in the middle of each potato.

④ Combine the beansprouts with the oil and seasoning and spoon in with the tomato.

⑤ Push the potato halves back together and place them in an ovenproof dish. Place the Mozzarella slices on top of each potato and return to the oven for about 5 minutes until the cheese has melted and the potatoes are hot.

⑥ Serve hot with a selection of salads.

PREPARATION TIME: 15 MINUTES
COOKING TIME: 1 HOUR 35 MINUTES

ASPARAGUS AND STILTON LAYER BAKE
—— SERVES 4 ——

	METRIC	IMPERIAL	AMERICAN
Butter, melted	50 g	2 oz	¼ cup
Large sheets of filo pastry (paste), fresh or thawed frozen	6	6	6
Can of asparagus spears, drained and chopped	350 g	12 oz	1 large
Stilton cheese, crumbled	175 g	6 oz	1½ cups
Pecan nuts, halved	75 g	3 oz	¾ cup
Balsamic vinegar	15 ml	1 tbsp	1 tbsp
Green peppercorns, roughly crushed	15 ml	1 tbsp	1 tbsp
Coarse salt			
Tomato and basil salad, to serve			

① Brush a large baking (cookie) sheet with butter.

② Take a sheet of the filo pastry and brush lightly with butter. Fold in half with the butter on the inside, place on the baking sheet and brush the top surface with more butter.

③ Repeat this process with two more sheets of pastry, laying them on top of the first sheet.

④ Scatter the asparagus over the surface of the top sheet of pastry, leaving a 1 cm/½ in border all the way round. Sprinkle the Stilton and nuts over the asparagus, then drizzle the balsamic vinegar over. Season with the crushed peppercorns and salt to taste.

⑤ Repeat the folding and buttering process with the remaining sheets of filo pastry and pile on top of the asparagus mixture, pressing down firmly around the edges to seal well.

⑥ Ensure that the surface has a good coating of the melted butter, then put in a preheated oven and cook at 200°C/ 400°F/gas mark 6 for about 15–20 minutes until crisp and golden.

⑦ Serve sliced, hot or cold, with a tomato and basil salad.

PREPARATION TIME: 15 MINUTES
COOKING TIME: 20 MINUTES

DESSERTS

The most fabulous desserts can be made with no cooking at all – the only ingredients you need are fresh fruit and cream and the rest is up to you. However, if you are feeling a little more adventurous, there are lots of new ideas here for you to create mouthwatering treats – with the minimum of washing up!

STRAWBERRY MOUNTAIN
—— SERVES 4 ——

	METRIC	IMPERIAL	AMERICAN
Fresh strawberries, hulled and quartered	350 g	12 oz	12 oz
Finely grated lemon rind	10 ml	2 tsp	2 tsp
Strawberry liqueur (or sweet sherry)	15 ml	1 tbsp	1 tbsp
Cottage cheese	350 g	12 oz	1½ cups
Soft cheese	100 g	4 oz	½ cup
Caster (superfine) sugar	100 g	4 oz	½ cup
Double (heavy) cream	120 ml	4 fl oz	½ cup
Powdered gelatine	10 ml	2 tsp	2 tsp
Lemon juice	45 ml	3 tbsp	3 tbsp
Oil, for greasing			
Extra strawberries, hulled, for decorating			

① Put the strawberries and lemon rind in a bowl with the liqueur and stir.

② Mix the cheeses together and beat in the sugar.

③ Whip the cream until thick and fold into the cheese mixture, then fold in the strawberry mixture.

④ Sprinkle the gelatine over the lemon juice in a small heatproof bowl, leave for a few minutes until spongy, then place the bowl in a pan of hot water and stir until dissolved. Cool, then fold into the cheese mixture.

⑤ Brush the inside of a pudding basin or bowl lightly with oil, then line with clingfilm (plastic wrap), smoothing it against the sides of the bowl.

⑥ Pour the mixture into the bowl, cover the surface with another piece of clingfilm, then place a saucer on top and a weight on top of this. Chill overnight.

⑦ Turn the dessert out on to an attractive serving plate and decorate with strawberries.

PREPARATION TIME: 30 MINUTES
COOKING TIME: NONE

PEACH AND ALMOND ICE CREAM

—— SERVES 4 ——

	METRIC	IMPERIAL	AMERICAN
Cans of peach slices, drained	2 x 410 g	2 x 14½ oz	2 large
Cans of evaporated milk	2 x 400 g	2 x 14 oz	2 large
Clear honey	30 ml	2 tbsp	2 tbsp
Caster (superfine) sugar	75 g	3 oz	⅓ cup
Ground almonds	100 g	4 oz	1 cup
Langues de chat biscuits (cookies), to serve			

① Place all the ingredients in a food processor or liquidiser and process until smooth.

② Pour into a plastic freezer container and place in the freezer until the ice cream is just starting to set around the edges.

③ Remove from the freezer, beat well and then return to the freezer and freeze until firm.

④ Transfer to the fridge for about 30 minutes before serving to allow it to soften enough to spoon out.

⑤ Serve in sundae glasses with langues de chat biscuits.

PREPARATION TIME: 10 MINUTES
COOKING TIME: NONE

CRÈME FRAÎCHE WITH CHRISTMAS FRUITS

—— SERVES 4 ——

	METRIC	IMPERIAL	AMERICAN
Can of black cherries, drained	400 g	14 oz	1 large
Raisins	75 g	3 oz	½ cup
Dates, stoned (pitted) and chopped	75 g	3 oz	½ cup
Sultanas (golden raisins)	50 g	2 oz	⅓ cup
Walnuts, roughly chopped	50 g	2 oz	½ cup
Blanched almonds, roughly chopped	50 g	2 oz	½ cup
Ground almonds	75 g	3 oz	¾ cup
Soft brown sugar	50 g	2 oz	¼ cup
Rum	15 ml	1 tbsp	1 tbsp
Ground cinnamon	2.5 ml	½ tsp	½ tsp
Grated nutmeg	2.5 ml	½ tsp	½ tsp
Crème fraîche	300 ml	½ pt	1¼ cups

Combine all the ingredients, then spoon into individual sundae glasses and chill well before serving.

PREPARATION TIME: 10 MINUTES

COOKING TIME: NONE

RICH CHOCOLATE ORANGE FLUMMERY

—— SERVES 4 ——

	METRIC	IMPERIAL	AMERICAN
Double (heavy) cream	300 ml	½ pt	1¼ cups
Mascarpone cheese	225 g	8 oz	1 cup
Icing (confectioners') sugar, sifted	15 ml	1 tbsp	1 tbsp
Grand Marnier	15 ml	1 tbsp	1 tbsp
Plain (semi-sweet) orange chocolate, grated	175 g	6 oz	1½ cups
Egg white	1	1	1
Cocoa (unsweetened chocolate) powder	5 ml	1 tsp	1 tsp
Finely pared strips of orange rind	10 ml	2 tsp	2 tsp

① Combine the cream, cheese, sugar and Grand Marnier and whisk until thick enough to hold its shape.

② Fold in the grated chocolate.

③ Whisk the egg white until stiff and fold into the cream mixture with a metal spoon. Divide the mixture between four sundae glasses and chill well.

④ Dust with the cocoa powder and serve topped with a few strips of orange rind.

PREPARATION TIME: 15 MINUTES
COOKING TIME: NONE

ICED APPLE AND ELDERFLOWER FOOL

—— SERVES 4 ——

	METRIC	IMPERIAL	AMERICAN
Cooking (tart) apples, peeled, cored and cut into pieces	450 g	1 lb	1 lb
Caster (superfine) sugar	75 g	3 oz	⅓ cup
Ready-made custard	150 ml	¼ pt	⅔ cup
Elderflower cordial	120 ml	4 fl oz	½ cup
Double (heavy) cream	150 ml	¼ pt	⅔ cup
Elderflowers, if available, to decorate			
Cigarettes Russes biscuits (cookies), to serve			

① Place the apples in a saucepan with the sugar and cover tightly. Simmer gently until the apples are very soft, then mash or liquidise to a purée.

② Allow to cool slightly, then stir in the custard and cordial.

③ Whip the cream until stiff, then fold into the cooled apple mixture.

④ Pour into a rigid freezer-proof container and freeze until just firm.

⑤ Spoon into iced sundae glasses, decorate with elderflowers (if you can find any in the hedgerow) and serve with Cigarettes Russes biscuits to accompany.

PREPARATION TIME: 15 MINUTES PLUS FREEZING TIME
COOKING TIME: 10 MINUTES

LIME MASCARPONE WITH COCONUT DESSERT

—— SERVES 4 ——

	METRIC	IMPERIAL	AMERICAN
Double (heavy) cream	150 ml	¼ pt	⅔ cup
Mascarpone cheese	225 g	8 oz	I cup
Grated zest and juice of 2 small limes			
Icing (confectioners') sugar, sifted	30 ml	2 tbsp	2 tbsp
Sweetened desiccated (shredded) coconut	60 ml	4 tbsp	4 tbsp
Toasted strands of coconut and lime twists, to decorate			

① Whip the cream until quite thick, then add the Mascarpone cheese and continue to beat until very thick.

② Stir in the lime zest and juice, the icing sugar and coconut. Spoon into sundae glasses and chill.

③ Serve topped with toasted coconut strands and a twist of lime.

PREPARATION TIME: 20 MINUTES

COOKING TIME: NONE

POACHED NECTARINES IN SWEET WINE
with MASCARPONE CREAM

—— SERVES 4 ——

	METRIC	IMPERIAL	AMERICAN
Cinnamon stick	I	I	I
Soft brown sugar	50 g	2 oz	¼ cup
Sweet white wine	300 ml	½ pt	1¼ cups
Brandy	90 ml	6 tbsp	6 tbsp
Water	150 ml	¼ pt	⅔ cup
Large nectarines, halved and stoned (pitted)	4	4	4
For the Mascarpone Cream:			
Mascarpone cheese	225 g	8 oz	I cup
Brandy	15 ml	I tbsp	I tbsp
Vanilla sugar	30 ml	2 tbsp	2 tbsp

① Place the cinnamon stick in a large saucepan with the brown sugar, wine, brandy and water.

② Heat gently and bring to the boil. Simmer for a few minutes, then add the nectarine halves.

③ Simmer gently for about 10 minutes until the fruit is tender.

④ To make the Mascarpone Cream, beat together all the ingredients to give a smooth consistency.

⑤ Serve the nectarines and syrup warm or cold with a helping of chilled Mascarpone Cream.

PREPARATION TIME: 10 MINUTES
COOKING TIME: 20 MINUTES

STRAWBERRY AND CURD CHEESE GALETTES

—— SERVES 4 ——

	METRIC	IMPERIAL	AMERICAN
Puff pastry (paste), fresh or thawed frozen	350 g	12 oz	12 oz
Curd cheese	100 g	4 oz	½ cup
Icing (confectioners') sugar, sifted	30 ml	2 tbsp	2 tbsp
Very large strawberries, cut lengthways into slices	4	4	4
Apple jelly (clear conserve), warmed	15 ml	1 tbsp	1 tbsp
Chilled cream, to serve			

① Roll out the pastry, cut four 13 cm/5 in circles and place on a baking (cookie) sheet. Score a line all the way round each circle about 5 mm/¼ in from the edge.

② Mix the curd cheese with the icing sugar and divide between the four circles, spreading out as far as the scored line.

③ Arrange the strawberry slices attractively over the cheese, then brush with the warm apple jelly.

④ Place in a preheated oven and cook at 220°C/425°F/gas mark 7 for 15–20 minutes until puffy and golden round the edges.

⑤ Serve warm or cold with chilled cream.

PREPARATION TIME: 10 MINUTES
COOKING TIME: 20 MINUTES

STEAMED BANANA AND PECAN NUT PUDDINGS

—— SERVES 4 ——

	METRIC	IMPERIAL	AMERICAN
A little oil, for greasing			
Butter, softened	100 g	4 oz	½ cup
Soft brown sugar	100 g	4 oz	½ cup
Eggs	2	2	2
Bananas, peeled and mashed	2	2	2
Shelled pecan nuts, roughly chopped	75 g	3 oz	¾ cup
Self-raising (self-rising) flour	100 g	4 oz	1 cup
A little milk			
Pouring cream, to serve			

① Oil and base-line four deep ramekins (custard cups) with greaseproof (waxed) paper.

② Cream the butter with the sugar until light and fluffy. Gradually beat in the eggs, then stir in the bananas and nuts. Fold in the flour with a metal spoon. Stir in enough milk to give a soft dropping consistency.

③ Divide the mixture between the ramekins, then cover each with a pleated piece of foil and secure by tying round a piece of string.

④ Place in a steamer and cover with a tight-fitting lid.

⑤ Steam over boiling water for 45 minutes, checking the water level in the steamer frequently and topping up when necessary.

⑥ Turn out the sponge puddings on to individual dishes and serve with fresh pouring cream.

PREPARATION TIME: 25 MINUTES
COOKING TIME: 45 MINUTES

PEAR AND ALMOND LAYER

—— SERVES 4 ——

	METRIC	IMPERIAL	AMERICAN
Butter, melted	100 g	4 oz	½ cup
Filo pastry (paste), fresh or thawed frozen	225 g	8 oz	8 oz
Can of pear halves, drained and finely chopped	400 g	14 oz	1 large
Ground almonds	100 g	4 oz	1 cup
Soft brown sugar	50 g	2 oz	¼ cup
Ground cinnamon	5 ml	1 tsp	1 tsp
Ground cloves	1.5 ml	¼ tsp	¼ tsp
Flaked (slivered) almonds	50 g	2 oz	½ cup
Finely grated lemon zest	5 ml	1 tsp	1 tsp
Butter, softened	50 g	2 oz	¼ cup
Clear honey, slightly warmed	45 ml	3 tbsp	3 tbsp
Crème fraîche, to serve			

① Use the melted butter to grease a roasting tin (pan) or dish about 30 × 20 × 5 cm/12 × 8 × 2 in.

② Place one pastry sheet in the base of the dish, cutting in half if necessary, and brush well with the melted butter. Repeat with nine more sheets of pastry to give a total of ten sheets.

③ Combine all the remaining ingredients except the honey and spread evenly over the pastry.

④ Cover the filling with ten more sheets of filo pastry, buttering each sheet well, particularly the top.

⑤ Using a sharp knife, cut right through the pastry and filling to make 16 7.5 × 5 cm/3 × 2 in rectangles.

⑥ Bake in a preheated oven at 190°C/375°F/gas mark 5 for about 20–25 minutes until crisp and golden. Allow to cool slightly then drizzle the honey over.

⑦ Serve hot or cold with crème fraîche.

PREPARATION TIME: 20 MINUTES
COOKING TIME: 25 MINUTES

GOOD AND EVIL
—— SERVES 4 ——

	METRIC	IMPERIAL	AMERICAN
Large bananas, thinly sliced	2	2	2
Greek yoghurt	120 ml	4 fl oz	½ cup
Honey	30 ml	2 tbsp	2 tbsp
Butter	25 g	1 oz	2 tbsp
Cocoa (unsweetened chocolate) powder	10 ml	2 tsp	2 tsp
Pecan nuts, roughly chopped	25 g	1 oz	¼ cup

① Divide the banana slices between four sundae glasses. Top with the Greek yoghurt.

② Place the honey, butter, cocoa powder and pecan nuts in a small saucepan and warm gently until the ingredients are melted and blended. Drizzle this sauce over the yoghurt and serve.

PREPARATION TIME: 10 MINUTES
COOKING TIME: 5 MINUTES

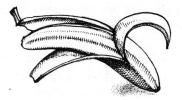

PATISSERIE BAKE WITH MANGO AND CHOCOLATE

—— SERVES 4 ——

	METRIC	IMPERIAL	AMERICAN
Butter	50 g	2 oz	¼ cup
Single (light) cream	300 ml	½ pt	1¼ cups
Eggs	2	2	2
Croissants, halved horizontally	4	4	4
Granulated sugar	50 g	2 oz	¼ cup
Can of mango slices, drained and roughly chopped	400 g	14 oz	1 large
Plain (semi-sweet) chocolate, coarsely grated	175 g	6 oz	1½ cups
Crème fraîche, to serve			

① Use a little of the butter to grease a fairly shallow ovenproof dish.

② Beat together the cream and eggs, then soak each croissant in the mixture for a few minutes and arrange in a single layer in the dish.

③ Sprinkle the sugar all over the surface, then dot with the remaining butter.

④ Place in a preheated oven and cook at 190°C/375°F/gas mark 5 for 20–30 minutes until the croissants are crisp and lightly browned.

⑤ Lay the chopped mango all over the top of the croissants, then sprinkle the grated chocolate over and return to the oven for about 10 minutes until the chocolate has melted and the fruit is hot.

⑥ Serve hot with crème fraîche.

PREPARATION TIME: 15 MINUTES
COOKING TIME: 40 MINUTES

OLD ENGLISH CHEESECAKE PACKETS
—— SERVES 4 ——

	METRIC	IMPERIAL	AMERICAN
For the dough:			
Egg	1	1	1
Water	15 ml	1 tbsp	1 tbsp
A pinch of salt			
Plain (all-purpose) flour	100 g	4 oz	1 cup
For the filling:			
Butter, very soft	15 ml	1 tbsp	1 tbsp
Curd cheese	100 g	4 oz	½ cup
Sugar	15 ml	1 tbsp	1 tbsp
Ground cinnamon	2.5 ml	½ tsp	½ tsp
Grated zest of 1 lemon			
Raisins	25 g	1 oz	2 tbsp
Soft brown sugar and diced butter, to serve			

① Make the dough by lightly beating the egg with the water, then stir in the salt with the flour. Bring together to form a dough, then place on a lightly floured board and roll out thinly to a square. Carefully cut out 6 cm/2½ in squares.

② Beat together all the filling ingredients.

③ Place a small spoonful of the filling mixture on the centre of each square and fold in half diagonally to give triangular parcels. Pinch the edges together.

④ Bring a pan of water to the boil and drop in the packets. When they rise to the surface, lift out with a draining spoon.

⑤ Serve while still hot sprinkled with soft brown sugar and dotted with butter.

PREPARATION TIME: 20 MINUTES
COOKING TIME: 5 MINUTES

COCONUT PANCAKES WITH MANGO SORBET

—— SERVES 4 ——

	METRIC	IMPERIAL	AMERICAN
Desiccated (shredded) coconut	25 g	1 oz	¼ cup
Plain (all-purpose) flour, sifted	75 g	3 oz	¾ cup
Egg	1	1	1
Canned coconut milk	150 ml	¼ pt	⅔ cup
Milk	150 ml	¼ pt	⅔ cup
Oil, for shallow-frying			
A tub of ready-made mango sorbet			
Toasted desiccated coconut, to decorate			

① Combine the coconut and flour in a mixing bowl. Make a well in the middle then break in the egg. Whisk the egg, then gradually beat in some of the flour and coconut mixture.

② Combine the coconut milk and milk, then gradually beat into the egg and flour mixture and whisk in the rest of the flour and coconut to give a smooth batter.

③ Heat a little oil in a frying pan (skillet) and pour in enough batter to cover the surface of the frying pan.

④ Cook until the batter dries and bubbles appear on the surface, then turn and cook the other side for a few minutes. Remove from the pan and keep hot while you cook the remaining pancakes.

⑤ Put a scoop of sorbet inside each hot pancake and serve decorated with toasted coconut.

PREPARATION TIME: 10 MINUTES
COOKING TIME: 15 MINUTES

ORANGE AND ALMOND DROPSIES

—— SERVES 4 ——

	METRIC	IMPERIAL	AMERICAN
Ground almonds	45 ml	3 tbsp	3 tbsp
Plain (all-purpose) flour	100 g	4 oz	1 cup
Caster (superfine) sugar	15 ml	1 tbsp	1 tbsp
Egg	1	1	1
Grated zest and juice of 1 orange			
Milk	200 ml	7 fl oz	scant 1 cup
Oil, for shallow-frying			
For the Orange Butter:			
Orange zest, grated	5 ml	1 tsp	1 tsp
Orange juice	10 ml	2 tsp	2 tsp
Soft brown sugar	15 ml	1 tbsp	1 tbsp
Butter, softened	100 g	4 oz	½ cup
Extra butter, to serve			

①   Combine the almonds, flour and caster sugar in a bowl and make a well in the centre. Break in the egg and whisk lightly to work in a little of the flour mixture.

②   Combine the orange zest, juice and milk (it may curdle but don't worry) and gradually beat into the egg and flour mixture, working everything together to create a smooth batter.

③   Heat a little oil in a frying pan (skillet) and drop 15 ml/ 1 tbsp quantities of the mixture into the pan, about three at a time.

④   When bubbles appear on the surface, turn over and cook the other sides for a few minutes.

⑤   Remove from the pan and keep hot while you cook the remaining batter in the same way.

⑥   Combine all the Orange Butter ingredients and work until quite smooth.

⑦   Serve the dropsies hot with 5 ml/1 tsp of the butter on top of each.

PREPARATION TIME: 15 MINUTES
COOKING TIME: 15 MINUTES

SPICED CRANBERRY COMPÔTE

—— SERVES 4 ——

	METRIC	IMPERIAL	AMERICAN
Cranberries	225 g	8 oz	8 oz
Eating (dessert) apples, peeled and diced	2	2	2
Fresh orange juice	60 ml	4 tbsp	4 tbsp
Port	60 ml	4 tbsp	4 tbsp
Water	150 ml	¼ pt	⅔ cup
Soft brown sugar	50 g	2 oz	¼ cup
Ground cinnamon	5 ml	1 tsp	1 tsp
A pinch of ground cloves			
Freshly grated nutmeg	2.5 ml	½ tsp	½ tsp
Crème fraîche	60 ml	4 tbsp	4 tbsp

① Place all the ingredients except the crème fraîche in a saucepan and bring slowly to the boil.

② Reduce the heat and simmer, stirring constantly, until the fruit is soft and the sauce is slightly thickened.

③ Ladle into individual sundae glasses, swirl in the crème fraîche and serve.

PREPARATION TIME: 5 MINUTES
COOKING TIME: 10 MINUTES

HOT STRAWBERRY FONDUE

—— SERVES 4 ——

	METRIC	IMPERIAL	AMERICAN
Ripe strawberries, hulled and roughly chopped	450 g	1 lb	1 lb
Caster (superfine) sugar	100 g	4 oz	½ cup
Water	15 ml	1 tbsp	1 tbsp
Lemon juice	15 ml	1 tbsp	1 tbsp
Whipping cream	150 ml	¼ pt	⅔ cup
Cubes of cake, langues de chat biscuits (cookies), sponge (lady) fingers and a selection of fresh fruits, cut into bite-sized pieces, to serve			

① Place the strawberries, sugar, water and lemon juice in a saucepan and heat gently until the strawberries are soft and the juices run.

② Transfer to a liquidiser or use a hand blender to liquidise the strawberry mixture.

③ Return to the heat and stir in the cream. Heat through but do not allow the mixture to boil.

④ Serve in a large warm bowl (or fondue pan if you have one) with the suggested accompaniments on small forks or cocktail sticks so that they can be dipped in the strawberry fondue.

PREPARATION TIME: 5 MINUTES
COOKING TIME: 5 MINUTES

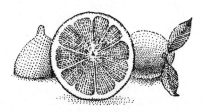

HIGHLAND BREAD AND BUTTER PUDDING

—— SERVES 4 ——

	METRIC	IMPERIAL	AMERICAN
Butter	75 g	3 oz	⅓ cup
Thin slices of white bread, crusts removed	8	8	8
Raspberry jam (conserve)	60 ml	4 tbsp	4 tbsp
Whisky	45 ml	3 tbsp	3 tbsp
Demerara sugar	50 g	2 oz	¼ cup
Single (light) cream	600 ml	1 pt	2½ cups
Eggs	2	2	2
Vanilla ice cream, to serve			

① Butter the bread, then spread with the jam. Cut each slice into four triangles.

② Arrange half the triangles in the bottom of an ovenproof dish and sprinkle over half the whisky and half the sugar. Place the remaining bread on the top and sprinkle on the rest of the whisky.

③ Beat together the cream and eggs and pour all over the bread.

④ Sprinkle the remaining sugar over the top. Leave to stand for about 30 minutes.

⑤ Place the dish in a roasting tin (pan) and pour in water to come half way up the side of the dish. Cook in a preheated oven at 180°C/350°F/gas mark 4 for about 30 minutes until puffy and golden.

⑥ Serve hot with a scoop of good-quality vanilla ice cream.

PREPARATION TIME: 15 MINUTES PLUS 30 MINUTES SOAKING TIME
COOKING TIME: 30 MINUTES

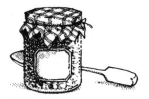

INDEX